य रहस्सेसु य निच्छप्प
पुच्छणिज्जे सयस्स वि ५
आलम्बणं चक्खू, मेढीभूय जाव सव्वकज्ज वड्ढावए याचि
होत्था ॥ ५ ॥

तस्स णं आणन्दस्स गाहावइस्स सिव न्दा नामं भारिया
होत्था, अहीण जाव सुरूवा। आणन्दस्स गाहावइस्स इट्ठा,
आणन्देणं गाहावइणा सद्धिं अणुरत्ता अविरत्ता इट्ठा, सद्ध
जाव पञ्चविहे माणुस्सए कामभोए पच्चणुभवमाणी विह
रइ ॥ ६ ॥

तस्स णं वाणियगामस्स बहिया उ रपुरत्थिमे दिसीभाए
एत्थ णं कोल्लाए नामं संनिवेसे होत्थ रिद्धत्थिमिय जाव
पासादिए ४ ॥ ७ ॥

तत्थ णं कोल्लाए संनिवेसे अ
मित्तनाइनियगसयणसंबंधिपरिजणे
अपरिभूए ॥ ८ ॥

गाहावइस्स बहुए
सद्द, अड्ढे जाव

page from the *Uvasa-
dasao*, one of the *Twelve
ngas* of the Jainist Scrip-
res written in Prakrit.

ding to *St. Luke*,
in the original
rgan Library).

the *Ko-ji-ki* or *Records
Matters* of the Shinto
hered under the Jap-
ial order in 712 A.D.

眞福寺本古事記の解題

眞福寺本古事記はその下卷の奥野によると龜山帝文永三年十二月中旬、神祇權大副大中
臣某が定世の孫の觀忠朝臣(從三位になる前とすれば元德三年以前か)から借りて二本に
別明(概大約寺本古になつたのは元德元年)し、一を家にとどめたのである。これより先きに
權大約宗賢右近衞大將慮原通躬卿が中卷を手に入れた爲がを記してゐる。これで眞福寺
所が、眞福寺本の賢營されたのは、上卷に「執筆賢瑜僧俗 卷」中卷に「執筆金剛資賢瑜
とあつて、この賢瑜といふ僧は、齊政友氏によると「同じ眞福寺に傳へたる秘藏寶繪の
應安第三天、十一月(山川孝雄博士の引用文には十二月とある)二十七日於尾州大須
金剛資賢瑜歲卅七
とあるによれば、」この眞福寺本古事記は上・中の二卷は北朝の應安四年(西紀一三七一)
卷は翌應安五年(西紀一三七二年)二十九歲の賢營であると知られる。先頃八代國治博十
た南朝の長慶帝の旨のものであるわけだ。ともかく古事記現存最古本の最古のものと云ま
六世紀宇も經て居り、弘長三年としても五世紀宇を經て居るのだから誤の多いのも無理
ても例を秘將までに摹げる
固(四)が固に、杯が桶に、偽が偽に、米が未又は末に、
に、沼が沽に、自が自に
に、杯が桶に、偽が偽に、米が末又は末に、那が邪に、懷が懷に、

SCHOOLCRAFT
COLLEGE LIBRARY

BL
29
.G27

Gaer, Joseph
Wisdom of the living religions

DATE DUE

BRADNER LIBRARY
SCHOOLCRAFT COLLEGE
LIVONIA, MICHIGAN 48152

SCHOOLCRAFT COLLEGE LIBRARY

3 3013 00004 5884

WITHDRAWN

The Wisdom of the

LIVING RELIGIONS

Other books by JOSEPH GAER

THE BURNING BUSH
THE UNCONQUERED
THE MAGIC FLIGHT
THE LORE OF THE OLD TESTAMENT
THE LORE OF THE NEW TESTAMENT
HEART UPON THE ROCK (A novel)
THE LEGEND CALLED MERYOM (A novel)
MEN AND TREES
FAIR AND WARMER
EVERYBODY'S WEATHER
HOLIDAY AROUND THE WORLD
YOUNG HEROES OF THE LIVING RELIGIONS
THE ADVENTURES OF RAMA (The *Ramayana*)
THE FABLES OF INDIA
HOW THE GREAT RELIGIONS BEGAN

The Wisdom of the

LIVING

RELIGIONS

BY JOSEPH GAER

DODD, MEAD & COMPANY
NEW YORK   1963

BL
29
.G27

FOURTH PRINTING

© 1956 BY JOSEPH GAER

ALL RIGHTS RESERVED

NO PART OF THIS BOOK MAY BE REPRODUCED IN ANY FORM
WITHOUT PERMISSION IN WRITING FROM THE PUBLISHER

LIBRARY OF CONGRESS CATALOG CARD NUMBER: 56-8362

PRINTED IN THE UNITED STATES OF AMERICA

APOLLO EDITION

PREFACE

Long before there was any written literature there already existed among many ancient nations a vast and complex oral literature. Its origin, we can only surmise, goes back to the beginning of man's unrecorded history when the need arose to communicate instruction to the young and to preserve it for subsequent generations. All early literature was a reservoir of accumulated folk wisdom which served the people as instruction on how, from past experience, to do things better; and what, from past experience, to avoid in order to prevent pain and disaster. And to fix this instruction in the mind of the young, the elders found it necessary to resort to a number of literary devices.

The gifted elders, in whose hands rested the responsibility of instruction, must have realized that when teaching by word rather than by exemplary deed, they were in need first and foremost of gaining and holding attention; and that this often devolved upon how the topic was presented—that it was a matter of literary form. Once attention was gained and held, the "lesson" they wished to impress had to be formulated in such a way that it would be grasped readily and firmly retained in the memory—again a matter of how the topic was formulated in words. To succeed in their objective, those early teachers related experiences of great importance to their audience, or, by their imaginative presentation, made the experiences appear of great importance. And the implications of the words had to be such that those who heard them would greatly benefit by remembering them. Finally, it was imperative for those who used only oral instruction to reduce the basic idea to a few words which, by their sense and form, would captivate the imagination and remain secure in the memory. This pedagogic need gave rise quite early to a great variety of literary forms, in which the fable, the allegory, the parable and the myth played a prominent part. And all these forms shared the characteristic of leading the mind of the listener to an inevitable conclusion.

Actually, the conclusion came first, for this was the object lesson. And the conclusion, which was the aim of the instruction, often took the form of a proverb or a saying. There is room for the argument that the earliest form of literary expression was the folk saying or proverb.

A common misconception exists that folklore in general, and the folk saying in particular, is an outgrowth of the mind of the people. Though all folk sayings have in common the quality of popularity, probably few were popularly conceived. The very popularity of the observations expressed in proverbs gives testimony to the fact that it was originated by a gifted observer, reflected upon by a profound mind and given expression by a witty tongue, even though the creator remained anonymous. Usually, the more popular and universally accepted a saying, the greater the individuality of the originator.

The saying is one of the earliest, if not the very earliest, form of literature; and it was widely recognized as one of the most effective vehicles that could be used to impress upon a people a moral code or an ethical system. This utilization of the saying in the teaching of morals and ethics came about quite naturally, since all teaching in ancient times was the responsibility of the priesthood; and every lesson became a religious lesson, and every conclusion, a moral conclusion. In early periods, when the shepherd was taught how to train and how to treat his newly domesticated shepherd dog, his lessons in this (as found in the sacred scriptures of Zoroastrianism) assumed a religious formulation and were presented as commandments directly from the Holy One, Ahura Mazda. Similarly, when people in subtropical zones were plagued by epidemics caused by fish or meat that seemed to spoil rapidly, observations were made as to which foods to avoid in order to prevent illness, and the injurious foods were prohibited to the people as religiously "unclean." This approach to instruction was manifested in all religions, early and late.

Since the priesthood was primarily concerned with the spiritual welfare of the people, their teachings were preponderantly devoted to ethical concepts of man's relation to man or to his God. Their teachings were almost invariably expressed in a highly stylized form, frequently in poetry, so that they could be remembered with ease. And in all religions we find a vast accumulation of sayings in a diversity of literary forms. In some religions the fable and the allegory is highly developed; in some the parable takes precedence over other forms; and some favor the proverb in gnomic poetry.

In all the sacred books of the world's religions we find (either distributed throughout or gathered into separate collections or both) treasuries of parables, fables, proverbs and precepts which have throughout the centuries retained their luster and kept their spiritual teachings alive, while the collections of early hymns, of priestly ritual and of sacrificial ceremonies have only a historical interest for us. There are the fables of Hinduism in the *Panchatantra* and the *Hitopadesa,* which are the source and inspiration of all the fablers in the literatures of the world; there is the *Dhammapada* of Buddhism, the parables of Christianity, the Analects of Confucianism, the Proverbs of Judaism, the *Hadith* or Table Talk of Mohammedanism and the *Tao-Te-King* of Taoism, all different forms of sayings, of unsurpassed profundity in the aggregate. In only one religion, Zoroastrianism, we find no collection of proverbs or sayings, and that is probably because the ancient books were completely destroyed by the followers of the religion that supplanted Zoroastrianism.

When we examine the sacred books of the living religions that have survived, we find that the precepts and sayings of each religion carry its fundamental teachings. And by their nature and number we can study the character of the people who created them. Some people, we find, have a greater aptitude than others for expressing themselves in proverbs. The Chinese, for example, are a people with a particular gift for the proverb. They have created so many that, it is claimed, a man may live to be a hundred without ever needing to communicate in anything but time-honored proverbs, regardless of time or circumstance. The Jews, too, from biblical times to the present, have exhibited a gift for expressing every variety of experience in a proverb; and there are a larger number of Jewish proverbs less than a century old than there are to be found in the Book of Proverbs. The lively imagination of the Arabs is reflected at its best in their proverbs; and it is interesting to note that even in their religious system there is greater ingenuity, perception and ethical probing in the proverbs of the *Hadith* (the approved collections of the Table Talk of Mohammed) than is to be found in the Koran.

The sayings of the living religions deserve study for a number of reasons. Each of the sayings is thought provoking, each contains a guiding principle and each is (in the original even if not always in the translation) expressed concisely, sharply, memorably. The aggregate sayings of any religion present us with the fundamental ethics of that religion. And a comparative study of the sayings of the world's religions reveals both the fundamental similarities in all religions and their differences.

The collections of proverbs in the literatures of the living religions is vast. Most of the sayings (and the term is used throughout in its broadest sense) are concerned with universal observations. But though preoccupied with basic and universal problems, the approach to them and to their solution differs. The differences in form often express significant differences of approach. In all the religions we find peace praised and war condemned; diligence approved and indolence denounced; good deeds held in higher esteem than right belief; charity extolled; theft, lying and covetousness held reprehensible, and so on. But the differences in the expression of approbation and disapprobation in each case reveal differences in temperament, in environment and in maturity. There are also a number of basic concepts on which different religions hold opposing views. Several religions extol monasticism, for example, whereas others disapprove of it, and one, Mohammedanism, flatly opposes it by the saying: "There is no room in Islam for monasticism."

To gather all the sayings of the living religions would result in a work of encyclopedic proportions, and is beyond the scope and objective of this book. A selection was made here of the characteristic sayings of each living religion. However, in the instance of some religions the examples are almost exhaustive for the particular collection—such as the parables of Jesus, the sayings of Buddha as given in the *Dhammapada*, the sayings of Confucius, as given in the Analects, and the sayings of the *Tao-Te-King*. Of other religions only a relatively small selection was possible because the original collections are so overwhelmingly large—such as the sayings of Hinduism, the Talmudic sayings of Judaism and the sayings of Mohammed. The sayings included here are those which give an idea of the contents of the sources used and their teachings.

Each group of sayings is preceded by a statement which briefs the reader on the religion it represents and the nature of the source or sources used. All the sayings are given in modern English. Difficult names and archaic terms were eliminated wherever possible. Also repetition of a precept or a principle, as found in practically all religions, was avoided excepting where the repetition gives shadings of difference in the moral conclusion.

A topical index is given on pages 297-324, alphabetically arranged, which shows at a glance how the same basic concepts are treated in the various religions, and it also enables the reader to compare the sayings on a given concept for their similarities and their differences.

The author is indebted to the following people who read the book in manuscript and made many helpful suggestions: Dr. Floyd H. Ross, Professor of World Religions, University of Southern California; Dr. Wayland D. Hand, Professor of German and Folklore, University of California in Los Angeles; Rev. Elton E. Shell, Librarian, School of Religion, University of Southern California;

Dr. Max Nussbaum, Rabbi of Temple Israel, Hollywood, California; Rabbi Alfred Wolf, Wilshire Boulevard Temple, Los Angeles, California; and Dr. Frank Sullivan, Professor of English, Loyola University of Los Angeles.

J. G.

Santa Monica, California,
January, 1956

Contents

xiii

The Sayings of

BUDDHISM

Hatred is not diminished by hatred
at any time. Hatred is diminished by
love—this is the eternal law.
(*Dhammapada*, 5)

BUDDHISM

Buddhism is a religion of introspection, of renunciation and compassion. The Buddhist seeks, first and foremost, to be at peace within himself. In no other religion is so much stress placed on the duty to find peace in one's own mind. The doctrine of what one must believe and do to attain this peace of mind is more elaborate in Buddhism than in any other religion. The duty to one's self does not lead to selfishness, for selfishness is the cause of all sorrow—a state to be deplored. It leads first to the renunciation of all extremes, then to the duty of selfless dedication to mankind. And this altruistic service to man can be rendered only by those who have reached the imperturbable state in which they accept both joy and sorrow, prosperity and adversity with equal calm. Buddhism requires its followers to be stoic in their approach to life.

The teachings of Buddhism are not presented as a revelation, to be accepted on faith, but the tenets are propounded in a logical system, which uses the familiar terms of propositions, inductions and syllogisms found in all systems of logic. Repeatedly in the Buddhist scriptures, after a statement is made it is immediately followed by, "What is the reason for that?" And then follows the reasoned explanation. Rarely is a reason given or an explanation made on a supernatural basis. Buddhism attempts to be completely rational. And it has been called, justifiably, the most philosophical of the living religions.

The basic tenets of Buddhism are given in The Twelve Links, The Four Noble Truths, The Eightfold Path, The

Ten Buddhist Commandments and in The Ten Perfections. The rest of the voluminous Buddhist scriptures are, essentially, an elaboration of those fundamental teachings.

Buddhism was born in India in the sixth century B.C. when the twenty-nine-year-old Prince Gautama renounced his life of luxury in the royal palace and went out as a beggar-monk to seek a solution to the riddle of life. After six years of search and meditation he finally found the answers he sought—and became The Enlightened One, the Buddha. The remaining forty-five years of his life he devoted to teaching and establishing his teachings within a system of logic. His discourses were preserved by his disciples in The Three Baskets of Wisdom (*Tipitaka*), which have since served as the sacred scriptures of Buddhism.

About three centuries after the Buddha's death, King Asoka and his son Mahendra established Buddhism as the state religion of India and introduced it in Ceylon. After that Buddhism spread to all parts of Asia and permeated Tibet, China, Korea and Japan. By the time Buddhism had almost completely disappeared from its birthplace, India, several centuries later, it had become firmly established in many other lands.

In the course of its migrations, and with the passing of the centuries, Buddhism went through many changes to meet new conditions and to adjust to new times. In the southern part of Asia, principally in Ceylon and Burma, Buddhism was retained in some of its early forms and is known as The Smaller Vehicle (*Hinayana*); in the north, principally in China and Japan, it grew into a complex system and is known as The Great Vehicle (*Mahayana*). These two, in turn, gave rise to many branches and sects.

Today approximately a fourth of the world's population are Buddhists. There are differences among them as great as one would find between the Roman Catholic and the Unitarian. Their differences do not lie in the essential principles but in their interpretations and methods of carrying them out.

To accept Buddhism, every Buddhist must, in a sense, pattern his own life after that of the Buddha: He must understand what caused Prince Gautama to make his great renunciation; he must observe with compassion the cycle of birth, aging, illness and death; he must try to reach enlightenment through altruistic dedication; he must find in meditation the essence of being and realize as it is stated in the Buddhist scriptures that "all that we are is the result of what we have thought; it is founded on our thoughts and is made up of our thoughts."

In the sayings of The Three Baskets of Wisdom the essentials of Buddhism are summarized.

DHAMMAPADA

The sacred scriptures of Buddhism, called The Three Baskets of Wisdom (*Tipitaka*), is the most voluminous and complex canonical work of any religion. The first and third Baskets or *Pitakas* are devoted to an elaborate and detailed description of the rules governing the monastic order, an explanation of how each rule was formulated and diverse commentaries on Buddhist doctrine. But in the second Basket—the *Sutta-Pitaka*—we find the great collection of Sermons and Discourses attributed to the Buddha, the treasury of The Five-Hundred-and-Fifty Birth-Stories of the Buddha—the famed *Jatakas*. Here, too, we find the Buddhist book of proverbs called the *Dhammapada*. Though the rest of the Buddhist scriptures are written partly in verse and partly in prose, the *Dhammapada* (which means The Path of Virtue or The Way of the Doctrine) is entirely in poetry. It consists of 423 stanzas, each presenting a precept or a principle; and, collectively, they contain an abstract of Buddhist ethics. For this reason, Buddhists often recommend the *Dhammapada* as a starting point for those who wish to gain an understanding of the ethics of their faith. And it was chosen here as the vehicle for the major ethical concepts of Buddhism.

The sayings from the *Dhammapada* are arranged in sequence, and the number in brackets after each saying corresponds to the original verse number. These sayings are better understood if one realizes that they are based upon the axiomatic acceptance of The Four Noble

6

Truths of Buddhism and other basic Buddhist precepts and commandments. The *Dhammapada* sayings are therefore preceded by The Twelve Links, The Four Noble Truths, The Eightfold Path and The Ten Buddhist Commandments, from the *Vinaya-Pitaka*, and The Ten Perfections, from the *Sutta-Pitaka*.

The Essence of BUDDHISM

1. THE TWELVE LINKS: THE BEGINNING OF ALL SORROW

Because of ignorance, there is individuality;
Because of individuality, there is intellect;
Because of intellect, there is separate name-and-form;
Because of name-and-form, there are the six senses;
Because of touch, there is sensation;
Because of sensation, there is craving;
Because of craving, there is grasping;
Because of grasping, there is individual existence;
Because of individual existence, there is earthly existence;
Because of earthly existence, there is decay and death.

Thus arises the chain of all grief and sorrow and despair.

(Vinaya-Pitaka; Maha-Vagga)

2. THE TWELVE LINKS: THE END OF ALL SORROW

With absolute cessation of ignorance, comes the end of individuality;
With the end of individuality, comes the end of intellect;
With the end of intellect, comes the end of separate name-and-form;

With the end of name-and-form, comes the end of the six senses;

With the end of the six senses, comes the end of contact;

With the end of contact, comes the end of the sense of touch;

With the end of touch, comes the end of craving;

With the end of craving, comes the end of grasping;

With the end of grasping, comes the end of individual existence;

With the end of individual existence, comes the end of earthly existence;

With the end of earthly existence, comes the end of decay and death.

Thus ends the chain of all grief and sorrow and despair.

(Vinaya-Pitaka; Maha-Vagga)

3. THE FOUR NOBLE TRUTHS

The First Noble Truth is that old age is suffering; illness is suffering; death is suffering; being exposed to what one dislikes is suffering; being separated from what one likes is suffering; failure to realize one's ambitions and desires is suffering.

The Second Noble Truth is that suffering comes from the desire for being which leads from birth to rebirth, together with lust and desire which finds gratification here and there; the desire for being, the desire for pleasure and the desire for power, these are the sources of suffering.

The Third Noble Truth is that suffering can be dissolved with the complete annihilation of desire, separating oneself from it and completely expelling it.

The Fourth Noble Truth is that the cessation of all desire can be gained by following the Eightfold Path.

(*Vinaya-Pitaka; Maha-Vagga*)

4. THE EIGHTFOLD PATH

Right Belief—that Truth is the guide of man;

Right Resolve—to be calm at all times and not to harm any living creature;

Right Speech—never to lie, never to slander anyone, and never to use coarse or harsh language;

Right Behavior—never to steal, never to kill, and never to do anything one may later regret or be ashamed of;

Right Occupation—never to choose an occupation that is considered bad;

Right Effort—always to strive for that which is good and avoid that which is evil;

Right Contemplation—of the Noble Truths, in calmness and detachment;

Right Concentration—will then follow and lead to the path of perfect peace.

(*Vinaya-Pitaka; Maha-Vagga*)

5. THE TEN BUDDHIST COMMANDMENTS

Do not destroy life.

Do not take what is not given you.

Do not commit adultery.

Tell no lies and deceive no one.

Do not become intoxicated.

Eat temperately and not at all in the afternoon.

Do not watch dancing, nor listen to singing or plays.

Wear no garlands, perfumes or any adornments.

Sleep not in luxurious beds.

Accept no gold or silver.

(The first five commandments all Buddhists must observe all the time; the last five they must observe on fast days. The monks must observe all of them all the time.)

(*Vinaya-Pitaka; Maha-Vagga*)

6. THE TEN PERFECTIONS

The first perfection is: *Giving.* As a full jar overthrown pours out the liquid and keeps back nothing, even so shall your charity be without reserve—as a jar overturned.

The second perfection is: *Duty.* As a yak-cow, when the hairs of her tail become entangled in anything, would rather suffer death than injury to her tail, even so should you keep your duty—as the yak to her tail.

The third perfection is: *Renunciation.* As a man in prison, suffering pain for long, knows that there is no pleasure for him but only to await release, so shall you look upon your existences on earth as prisons, and turn your face toward renunciation and await release.

The fourth perfection is: *Insight.* As the beggar-monk shuns no families from whom he begs, whether lowly or high or in between, and acquires his daily fare, so shall you at all times question the wise and gain insight.

The fifth perfection is: *Courage.* As the lion, king of beasts, whether when lying down or standing up, lacks no courage, but is ever high-hearted, so also shall you in each of your individual-existences hold fast to your courage.

The sixth perfection is: *Patience.* As the earth bears all that is cast upon it, both the pure and the impure, and feels no resentment nor rejoicing, so also shall you receive favors and rebuffs alike with indifference.

The seventh perfection is: *Truth.* As the star of healing is balanced in the heavens, and swerves not from its path in its time and its season, so also shall you remain fixed on your path of truth.

The eighth perfection is: *Resolution.* As the stone mountain, firmly based, quails not before the tempest, but abides in its place, so also shall you abide in your resolution once resolved.

The ninth perfection is: *Lovingkindness.* As water quenches the thirst of the good and the bad alike, and cleanses them of dust and impurity, so also shall you treat your friend and your foe alike with lovingkindness.

The tenth perfection is: *Serenity.* As indeed the earth looks with serenity on all the pure and impure that are cast upon it, even so shall you approach with serenity both joy and sorrow—if you are to attain wisdom.

Thus many are the things which in this world make wisdom perfect; beyond these there are no others.

(Sutta-Pitaka; Buddha-Vasma)

The Sayings of the
DHAMMAPADA

1a. All that we are is the result of what we have thought: it is founded on our thoughts and is made up of our thoughts. (1)

2a. If a man speaks or acts with an evil thought, pain follows him, as the wheel follows the foot of the ox that draws the cart; if a man speaks or acts with a pure thought, happiness follows him, as the shadow that never leaves him. (2-4)

3a. Hatred is not diminished by hatred at any time. Hatred is diminished by love—this is the eternal law. (5)

4a. Those who remember that we must come to an end in this world, their quarrels cease at once. (6)

5a. He who lives for pleasures only, his senses uncontrolled, will be overthrown by *Mara* (Temptation), as the wind throws down a rootless tree. He who lives without looking for pleasures, his senses well-controlled, will not be overthrown by *Mara* (Temptation), as the wind cannot move a mountain of stone. (7-8)

6a. He who wishes to put on the cloak of the monk without first cleansing himself of sin, is unworthy of the cloak. (9)

7a. Those who imagine truth in untruth, and see untruth in truth, never arrive at truth but follow vain desires. (11)

8a. As rain breaks through an ill-thatched roof, so lust breaks through an ill-trained mind. (13)

9a. The evildoer mourns in this world, and he mourns in the next—he mourns in both. He mourns and suffers when he sees the evil results of his own deeds. (15)

10a. The virtuous man delights in this world, and he delights in the next—he delights in both. He delights and rejoices when he sees the good results of his own work. (16)

11a. The thoughtless man, though versed in the Doctrine but not a doer of it, has no share in the religious life, but is like a cowherd counting the cows of others. (19)

12a. Thoughtfulness is the road to immortality (*Nirvana*); thoughtlessness, the road to death. (21)

13a. The thoughtful do not die; the thoughtless are as if dead already. (21)

14a. The wise who are meditative, steady, and always exerting strong powers, attain to *Nirvana*, the highest happiness. (23)

15a. By thoughtfulness, by restraint and self-control, the wise man may make for himself an island which no flood can overwhelm. (25)

16a. Fools follow vanity; but the wise man prizes his thoughtfulness as a treasure. (27)

17a. Thoughtful among the thoughtless, and awake among slumberers, the wise man advances like a racer. (29)

18a. By thoughtfulness did Indra (god of the firmament and the rain) rise to the lordship of the gods. (30)

19a. People always praise thoughtfulness; blame thought-lessness. (30)

20a. A monk who delights in thoughtfulness and fears thoughtlessness is close to *Nirvana*. (32)

21a. As the arrow-maker makes straight his arrow, so the wise man makes straight the trembling and unsteady thought which is difficult to control and difficult to hold back. (33)

22a. As fish taken from the waters and placed on dry ground, so our thought trembles all over in its effort to escape the dominion of temptation. (34)

23a. It is good to tame the mind, which is difficult to control and is flighty, rushing wherever it lists; a tamed mind brings happiness. (35)

24a. It is good to tame the mind and to guard one's thoughts; a tamed mind and thoughts well guarded bring happiness. (35-36)

25a. If a man's faith is unstable and his peace of mind troubled, his knowledge will not be perfect. (38)

26a. Man, whose body is as fragile as a jar, should make his thoughts firm as a fortress. (40)

27a. Whatever a hater may do to the one he hates, or an enemy to an enemy, a misdirected mind will suffer greater mischief. (42)

28a. He who knows that his body is like froth and as un-substantial as a mirage, will break the flower-tipped arrow of the Great Tempter and never see the King of Death (46)

29a. Death carries off a man who is gathering flowers and whose mind is distracted as a flood carries off a sleeping village. (47)

30a. As the bee collects nectar and departs without injuring the flower or its color or scent, so let the sage go about a village. (49)

31a. Like a beautiful flower full of color but without scent are the fair words of him who himself does not act accordingly. (51)

32a. The scent of flowers does not travel against the wind; but the fragrance of good people travels even against the wind. (54)

33a. Even upon a heap of rubbish the lotus will grow full of sweet perfume and delight; even so the true disciple of the enlightened Buddha will shine forth among the people who walk in darkness. (58)

34a. Long is the night to him who is wakeful; long is the mile to him who is tired; long is life to the foolish who do not know the true law. (60)

35a. If a traveler does not meet with one who is better or his equal, let him travel alone; for there is no companionship with a fool. (61)

36a. "These sons belong to me and this wealth belongs to me"—with such thoughts the fool tries to console himself. He himself does not belong to himself, how much less his sons and wealth! (62)

37a. The fool who knows his foolishness is wise to that extent. (63)

38a. A fool may associate with a wise man all his life, but perceive the truth as little as the spoon perceives the taste of soup. An intelligent man may associate with a wise man one minute, and perceive the truth as the tongue perceives the taste of soup. (64-65)

39a. The deed of which a man must repent, and the results of which he receives with tears, is not well done; the deed which a man does not repent, and the results of which he receives with joy, is well done. (67-68)

40a. As long as the evil deed done does not bear fruit, the fool thinks it is like honey; but when it ripens then he suffers. (69)

41a. An evil deed, like freshly drawn milk, does not turn sour at once. (71)

42a. The knowledge that a fool acquires, far from profiting him, destroys his good fortune and cleaves his head. (72)

43a. The fool wishes for precedence among the monks, for lordship in the monasteries, for honor among other people. (73)

44a. If you meet a man who can show you what is to be avoided and knows how to administer reproof, follow him as you would follow a man who can reveal hidden treasures. (76)

45a. As the irrigators direct water wherever they like, and the arrow-makers bend the arrow, so the wise control themselves. (80)

46a. As a solid rock is not shaken by the wind, so the wise man does not waver before blame or praise. (81)

47a. Whether touched by happiness or sorrow, the wise man never appears elated or depressed. (83)

48a. If, whether for his own sake or for the sake of others, a man neither wishes for a son, nor wealth, nor lordship, and if he does not wish for any success by unfair means, he is a good and wise man. (84)

49a. Few there are among men who arrive at the other shore; most of them run up and down this shore. (85)

50a. Those whose minds are well-grounded in the seven elements of knowledge, who cling to nothing with rejoicing, who curb their appetites and are full of light, they gain *Nirvana* even in this world. (89)

51a. There is no suffering for him who has finished his journey and abandoned grief. (90)

52a. Even the gods envy the man whose senses have been subdued, like horses well broken in by the driver, and who is free from pride and evil propensities. (94)

53a. His thoughts are quiet, his words and deeds are quiet, he who has become a quiet man. (96)

54a. Even though a speech may have a thousand words, but is made up of nonsense, one word of sense is better, which, if a man hears it, he becomes quiet. And even though a poem have a thousand stanzas, but is made up of nonsense, one stanza is better, which, if a man hears it, he becomes quiet. (100-102)

55a. Though a man go out to battle a thousand times against a thousand men, if he conquers himself he is the greater conqueror. (103)

56a. Not even a god can change into defeat the victory of a man who has vanquished himself. (105)

57a. Though a man tends the sacrificial fire in the forest for a hundred years, and if he but for one moment pays homage to the man whose soul is grounded in true knowledge, better is that moment of homage than the hundred years of sacrifice. (106)

58a. The man who habitually respects the aged, will have four things increased to him: life, beauty, happiness and power. (109)

59a. He who lives to be a hundred years without perceiving the highest law, a life of one day is better for him if he perceives the highest law. (115)

60a. The man who does good slothfully, his mind delights in evil. (116)

61a. If a man commits a sin, let him not do it again; let him not delight in it, for the accumulation of evil is painful. (117)

62a. If a man does what is good, let him do it again; let him delight in it, for the accumulation of good is delightful. (118)

63a. Even a good man sees evil days as long as good deeds bear no fruit; but when his good deeds ripen, then does the good man see good days. (120)

64a. Even if the water falls drop by drop, it will fill the pot; and the fool will become full of evil, even though he gathers it little by little. (122)

65a. Let a man avoid evil deeds as a man who loves life avoids poison. (123)

66a. He who has no wound on his hand may touch poison with it; poison does not affect one who has no wound, nor can evil touch one who does not commit evil. (124)

67a. If a man offend an innocent person, the evil will fall back upon that fool like light dust thrown up against the wind. (125)

68a. Not in the sky, not in the midst of the sea, not even in the clefts of the mountains is there a spot in the whole world where, if a man abide there, death could not overtake him. (128)

69a. All men tremble at punishment and all men fear death; remember that you are like them and do not kill nor cause slaughter. (129)

70a. He who in seeking happiness causes pain to others, who also long for happiness, will not find happiness after death. (131)

71a. Do not speak harshly to anyone; for those who are spoken to will answer you in the same way. (133)

72a. As the cowherd with his staff drives his cows into a stable, so do age and death drive the living. (135)

73a. A fool does not know what awaits him when he commits his evil deeds. (136)

74a. Not nakedness, not matted locks, not dirt or fasting or sleeping on the bare earth, or sitting motionless can purify a man who has not overcome his doubts. (141)

75a. Is there in this world a man so restrained by modesty that he can bear reproof as a well-trained horse the whip? (143)

76a. How can there be laughter, how can there be joy in this world that is always burning? (146)

77a. After a stronghold has been made of the bones and it is covered with flesh and blood, there come to dwell in it old age and death, pride and deceit. (150)

78a. A man who has learned little grows old like an ox; the flesh grows but his knowledge does not grow. (152)

79a. Men who have not led a religious life and have not laid up for themselves a treasure in their youth, die like herons on a lake without fish. (155)

80a. One's own self is the most difficult to subdue. (159)

81a. Self is the lord of self. (160)

82a. The evil done by one's self, born by one's self, begotten by one's self, crushes the foolish as a diamond breaks even hard stones. (161)

83a. By oneself evil is done; no one can defile or purify another. (165)

84a. The pure and impure stand and fall by their own deeds; no one can purify another. (165)

85a. Let a man after he has discerned his duty be faithful to his duty. (166)

86a. Look upon the world as you would on a bubble, look upon it as on a mirage: the king of death does not see him who thus looks upon the world. (170)

87a. Look upon this world, glittering like a royal chariot! The fools are immersed in it; but the wise are not attached to it. (171)

88a. He whose evil deeds are covered by good deeds brightens up the world, like the moon when freed from clouds. (173)

89a. The liar and the scoffer, there is no evil he will not commit. (176)

90a. Better than lordship over the earth, better than going to heaven, is the reward of the first step toward holiness. (178)

91a. Even the gods envy those who are awakened and not forgetful, who are given to meditation, who are wise, and who delight in the repose of retirement from this world. (181)

92a. Difficult to obtain is birth in human form, difficult is the life of mortals, difficult is the hearing of the True Law, difficult is the attainment of Buddhahood. (182)

93a. Not to commit sin, to do good, and to purify one's mind, that is the teaching of the Awakened. (183)

94a. Not to blame, not to strike, to be moderate in eating, to sleep and sit alone, and to dwell on the highest thoughts—this is the teaching of the Awakened. (185)

95a. Lust will not be satisfied even by a shower of gold. (186)

96a. Men, driven by fear, go to many refuges—to the mountains, to the forests, to groves of sacred trees—but none delivers him from his pains. But he who takes refuge with Buddha—who sees the Four Holy Truths and follows the Eightfold Holy Path—he will be delivered from pain. (188-189)

97a. A Buddha is not easily found; he is not born everywhere. (193)

98a. He who pays homage to those who deserve homage, his merit cannot be measured by anyone. (195)

99a. We live happily, indeed, among men who hate us, free of hatred; among men who are ailing, free from ailments; among men who are greedy, free from greed. Though we call nothing our own, we shall be like the bright gods, feeding on happiness. (197-199)

100a. Victory breeds hatred. He who has given up both victory and defeat, he is contented and happy. (201)

101a. There is no fire like passion; there is no evil like hatred; there is no pain like this body; there is no happiness greater than peace. (202)

102a. Hunger is the worst of diseases, and the body the chief source of sorrow. He who understands this well, knows that *Nirvana* is the highest happiness. (203)

103a. Health is the greatest of gifts and contentment the best of riches. (204)

104a. He who has tasted the sweetness of solitude and tranquillity becomes free from fear and free from sin. (204-205)

105a. Company with fools, as with an enemy, is always painful; company with the wise is like the meeting with kinfolk. (207)

106a. One should follow the good and the wise, as the moon follows the path of the stars. (208)

107a. He who gives himself to vanity, and does not give

himself to meditation, will in time envy him who has exerted himself in meditation. (209)

108a. Not to see what is pleasant is pain, and it is pain to see what is unpleasant. (210)

109a. From pleasure come grief and fear; he who is free from pleasure knows neither grief nor fear. (212)

110a. From lust come grief and fear; he who is free from lust knows neither grief nor fear. (213)

111a. Kinsmen, friends and lovers (well-wishers) salute a man who has been away for a long time and returns safe from afar; likewise his good works receive a man when he comes from this world to the other. (219-220)

112a. Let a man put away anger, forsake pride, and overcome all bondage. (221)

113a. No suffering befalls the man who calls nothing his own. (221)

114a. He who holds back rising anger like a rolling chariot is a real driver; others are but holding the reins. (222)

115a. Let a man overcome anger by love, let him overcome evil by good, let him overcome greed with liberality and lies with truth. (223)

116a. By these three steps you will come near to the gods: speak the truth; do not yield to anger; give even though you have but a little to give. (224)

117a. There is an old saying: They blame him who sits silent; they blame him who speaks much; they blame him who says little. There is no one in the world who does not get blamed. (227)

118a. There never was, there never will be, nor is there now a man who is always blamed, or a man who is always praised. (228)

119a. Beware of the anger of the tongue, and control your tongue. Beware of the anger of the mind, and control your mind. (231)

120a. Make yourself an island, work hard, be wise. When your impurities are blown away and you are free from guilt, you will enter into the world of the elect. (236)

121a. As rust sprung from iron eats into its own source, so do their own deeds bring sinners to an evil end. (240)

122a. There is a taint worse than all taints, and its name is ignorance. (243)

123a. Life is easy to live for a man who is without shame, bold as a crow, a mischief-maker, insulting, arrogant and dissolute. But life is hard to live for a man who is modest, always looks for what is pure, free from attachment, unassuming, and clear of vision. (244-245)

124a. He who destroys life, speaks untruth, takes what is not given him, goes in to another's wife, and the man who drinks intoxicating liquors, he, even in this world digs up his own roots. (246-247)

125a. People give according to their faith or according to their pleasure. (249)

126a. The fault of others is easily perceived, but that of one's self is difficult to perceive. A man winnows his neighbor's faults like chaff, but hides his own, even as a cheat hides an unlucky cast of the die. (252)

127a. If a man looks for the faults in others and is forever inclined to take offense, his own passions will grow and he is far from the destruction of passion. (253)

128a. A man is not learned because he talks much. (258)

129a. A man is not an elder because his head is gray. (260)

130a. An envious, parsimonious, deceitful man does not become respectable merely by the beauty of his complexion. (262)

131a. By clipping his hair an undisciplined man who speaks falsehood does not become a monk. (264)

132a. A man is not a mendicant simply because he asks for alms. (266)

133a. A man is not a sage simply because he observes silence. (268)

134a. The best of paths is the Eightfold Path; the best of truths are the Four Noble Truths; the best of states is the passionless state; the best of men is he who has eyes to see. (273)

135a. You yourself must make the effort. The Buddhas are only teachers. (276)

136a. All created things perish; he who knows and sees this is at peace in a world of pain. All existing things in this world are unreal; he who knows and sees this is beyond the thrall of grief. (277-279)

137a. He who does not waken when it is time to rise and, who though young and strong, is full of sloth, whose will and thought are weak, that lazy and idle man will not attain to wisdom. (280)

138a. Through meditation wisdom is won; through lack of meditation wisdom is lost. The man who knows this twofold path of gain and loss thus may place himself that wisdom may grow. (282)

139a. Cut down the whole forest of desire, not just one tree only. (283)

140a. So long as the desire of a man toward women is not destroyed, so long his mind is in bondage, as the nursing calf is to its mother. (284)

141a. "Here I shall dwell in the winter and summer, here I shall dwell in the rain"—so the fool thinks, but does not think of death. (286)

142a. Death comes and carries off a man, as a flood carries off a sleeping man. (287)

143a. Sons are of no help, nor a father, nor relatives; there is no help from kinfolk for the one whom death has seized. (288)

144a. If by leaving a small pleasure one sees a great pleasure, the wise man will leave the small pleasure to look at the great. (290)

145a. He who, by causing pain to others, wishes to obtain pleasure for himself, will become entangled in bonds of hatred and will never be free from hatred. (291)

146a. What ought to be done remains undone; what ought not to be done is done; thus the desires of the unruly and thoughtless people are forever increasing. (292)

147a. The disciples of the Buddha are always awake; and their minds day and night delight in meditation. (297)

148a. It is painful to dwell with unequals. (302)

149a. Good people shine from afar, like the peaks of the Himalayas. (304)

150a. Four things befall the man who courts his neighbor's wife; first, acquisition of demerit; second, an uncomfortable bed; third, evil report; and lastly, hell. (309)

151a. There is the short pleasure of the frightened in the arms of the frightened; then comes the long punishment of the law. Therefore let no man think of his neighbor's wife. (310)

152a. A lax ascetic only scatters the dust of passion more widely. (313)

153a. Those who fear when they ought not to fear, and fear not when they ought to, such men, embracing a false doctrine, enter the downward path. (317)

154a. Those who know what is forbidden as forbidden, and what is not forbidden as not forbidden, such men, embracing the true doctrine, enter the good path. (318)

155a. Endure abuse patiently as the elephant in battle endures the arrow sent from the bow. (320)

156a. The elephant does not eat a morsel when bound, but longs for the elephant grove. (324)

157a. This mind of mine went formerly wandering about as it liked, as it listed, as it pleased; but I shall hold it now firmly, as the rider who wields the hook holds in the furious elephant. (326)

158a. If a man finds no prudent companion to walk with, no one who is upright and steadfast, let him walk alone like a king who has left his conquered country, like an elephant in the forest. (329)

159a. It is better to live alone, for there is no companionship in a fool. (330)

160a. Pleasant in this world is the state of a mother, pleasant is the state of a father, pleasant is the state of an ascetic. (332)

161a. Pleasant is virtue that lasts to old age, pleasant is the faith firmly rooted; pleasant is the attainment of intelligence, pleasant is the avoiding of sin. (333)

162a. The passion of a heedless man grows like a creeper, and he runs from life to life, like a monkey seeking fruit in the forest. (334)

163a. He who overcomes his fierce desire is difficult to conquer in this world; suffering falls from him like rain drops from a lotus leaf. (336)

164a. As a tree though cut down grows up again as long as its roots are sound and firm, even so the man whose thirst has not been destroyed will suffer pain again and again. (338)

165a. Men driven by thirst run about like the hunted hare. (343)

166a. The wise man does not call that a strong fetter which is made of iron or wood or hemp; far stronger is the passionate devotion to sons and wives and to precious jewelry. (345)

167a. Those who are immersed in lust run down the stream of desires like a spider runs down the web which he himself has spun. (347)

168a. Give up what is before, give up what is behind, and give up what is between when you go to the Other Shore.

If your mind is altogether free you will not again enter into birth and decay. (348)

169a. If a man is tossed by doubts and swayed by strong passions and yearning only for what is delightful, his desires will grow and make his fetters strong. (349)

170a. He who is without desire and without attachment and who understands the words of the ancients is truly wise; he has received his last body. (352)

171a. The gift of the Law exceeds all gifts; the sweetness of the Law exceeds all sweetness; the delight in the Law exceeds all delight; the extinction of all desire overcomes all suffering. (354)

172a. By the thirst for riches the foolish man destroys himself as if he were his own enemy. (355)

173a. As the fields are damaged by weeds, mankind is damaged by lust, hatred and delusion. Therefore a gift bestowed on those who are free from lust, hatred and delusion brings a great reward. (356)

174a. Restraint in the eye is good, good is restraint in the ear; restraint in the nose is good, good is restraint in the tongue. Restraint in the body is good, better is restraint in the mind. Restraint in all things is good. The monk, restrained in all things, is freed from all pain. (360-361)

175a. He who controls his hand, he controls his feet; he who controls his speech, he who delights inwardly, who is calm, who is solitary and content, him they call a monk. (362)

176a. The monk who controls his mouth and teaches the meaning of the Law, his words are sweet. (363)

177a. O monk, do not overrate what you have received, nor ever envy others; a monk who envies others does not obtain peace of mind. (365)

178a. He who does not grieve over what is no more is indeed a monk. (367)

179a. Without knowledge there is no meditation; without meditation there is no knowledge. He who has knowledge and meditation is near to *Nirvana*. (372)

180a. As the jasmine sheds its withered flowers, even so men should shed lust and hatred. (377)

181a. Rouse yourself by yourself, examine yourself by yourself; thus self-guarded and protected will you live happily, O monk. (379)

182a. Curb yourself as the merchant curbs a noble horse. (380)

183a. The young monk who applies himself to Buddha's teachings lights up this world like the moon freed from clouds. (382)

184a. He, indeed, is a member of the highest caste (*brahmana*) who, after cutting the strap and the thong, the rope with all that pertains to it, has destroyed all obstacles and is awakened. (387)

185a. He, indeed, is a *brahmana* who is free from anger, dutiful, virtuous, without appetites, who is subdued and has received his last body. (389)

186a. He, indeed, is a *brahmana* who does not hurt any creature, whether feeble or strong, who does not kill nor cause slaughter. (405)

187a. He, indeed, is a *brahmana* who is tolerant among the intolerant, gentle among the violent, and free from greed among the greedy. (406)

188a. He, indeed, is a *brahmana* who has no longings as a result of knowledge, is free from doubt, and who has immersed himself in the Immortal. (411)

189a. He, indeed, is a *brahmana* who calls nothing his own, whether it pertains to past, present or future, who is poor and free from grasping. (421)

JATAKAS

Nearly a third of the Buddhist scriptures is devoted to stories and fables, each intended to teach a moral lesson, and all based upon events in the many reincarnations of the Buddha. The stories are known as Birth-Stories or *Jatakas*. There are, in tradition if not in fact, 550 of these Birth-Stories, all presented in a highly stylized form. Each begins with an event in the life of the Buddha told in the present, which becomes the occasion for recalling an event in a former life of the Buddha when he was the *Bodisat* or the Buddha-to-be. The stories or fables are given in prose, but end with a conclusion, drawn by the *Bodisat*, in poetry. As the Birth-Stories progress the conclusions become very complex and the verses in which they are given grow progressively in number.

While it is not necessary to read the stories and fables to understand the conclusions given in the gnomic couplets, the conclusions alone give the reader no idea of the delightful character and literary structure of these Birth-Stories. And those interested in reading them will find a list of several collections of *Jatakas* given in the bibliography at the end of this book. Here a selection of one hundred conclusions of the *Bodisat* are presented; and the number at the end of each saying refers to the number of the Birth-Story in the Pali canon, as given in the six volumes of the *Jatakas*, edited by Professor E. B. Cowell.

Sayings from the
JATAKAS

1b. As they who dig deep and untiringly even in the sand will find water, so the wise in perseverance strong find in their hearts peace. (2)

2b. In lust, in anger and in delusion lies the real impurity, and not in dirt. (4)

3b. From the humblest start and with trifling capital will the able man rise to wealth, even as his breath can nurse a flame. (4)

4b. They reap their hearts' desire who hurry not. (8)

5b. The man who guards not, nor is guarded, lives happy, freed from slavery to lusts. (10)

6b. The upright kindly man has his reward. (11)

7b. Cursed be the dart of love that causes pain; cursed be the land ruled by women; cursed be the fool who bows to woman's sway. (13)

8b. There is nothing viler in this world than the lust of taste. (14)

9b. Pluck out self-love as with the hand you pluck the autumn water-lily, and you will set your heart on the perfect path of peace. (25)

10b. Speak only words of kindness; never words unkind. (28)

11b. The poor birds shall not through me from out their nests be torn. (31)

12b. Where agreement reigns, the birds carry off the net; when discord rises among them, they all fall prey into the net. (33)

13b. They who honor age are versed in truth. (37)

14b. The good man thinks his goodness is but sin so long as it ripens not to fruit. (40)

15b. Far rather headlong plunge into the gulf of hell than stoop to shame. (40)

16b. The headstrong man who pays no heed to friendly counsel shall come to certain harm. (41)

17b. Foolish friends are worse than wise enemies. (44)

18b. Knowledge crowns endeavor with success. (47)

19b. Misguided effort leads to loss, not gain. (48)

20b. The fool waits for "lucky days" but luck always misses him. (49)

21b. When gladness fills the heart and fills the mind, and when righteousness is practiced to win peace, he who so walks shall gain the victory and all fetters utterly destroy. (56)

22b. Go not too far, but learn to shun excess; for overblowing lost what blowing won. (60)

23b. It is nature's law that rivers wind, trees grow wood, and, given the opportunity, women work iniquity. (62)

24b. Like a kingless kingdom, like a stream run dry, so is a woman, who, though she has ten brothers, has no mate. (67)

25b. Tasks deferred in joy are done at last in tears. (71)

26b. Ingratitude lacks more, the more it gets. (72)

27b. The storm overthrows the solitary tree. (74)

28b. A friend is he who seven steps will go to help us; twelve attest the comrade true. (83)

29b. Naught can compare with goodness. (87)

30b. Speak kindly, revile not your fellow men; love kindness, reviling breeds sorrow. (88)

31b. How plausible the story the rascal told! How heedful of the straw! How heedless of the gold! (89)

32b. Trust not the trusted, nor the untrusted trust— through trust the lion bit the dust. (93)

33b. "Wise" rightly, "Wisest" wrongly got his name. (98)

34b. If you are wise you will not linger among enemies. (103)

35b. Too often you tried: clearing the four javelins, upon the fifth you died. (116)

36b. Let great and small and equals all do their best. (121).

37b. What brings me weal, may bring you woe. (126)

38b. You may ail or eat—you cannot do both. (130)

39b. Give food to one cat and soon a second appears. (137)

40b. Matted hair and a garment of skin do not make an ascetic. (138)

41b. Once bitten, twice shy. (148)

42b. If poison lurk in the sapling, what will the full-grown tree prove to be? (149)

43b. Nothing is better than good company; nothing is worse than bad company. (162)

44b. The heart that boundless pity feels for all things that have birth, in such a heart nothing narrow or confined can ever be. (169)

45b. There is no tribe of animals but it has its virtuous ones—see how the wretched monkey stands worshipping the sun! (175)

46b. Given the proper groom, the horse will quickly learn. (184)

47b. Muddy water will not show the fish or shells below; and so with clouded wit. (185)

48b. Even a broken bowstring can be mended; forgive your wife and cherish not the anger in your heart. (191)

49b. "I like not this" and "I like not that" he cries who stands beside the granary and cannot pay. (199)

50b. No iron fetters bind so hard as passion and the love of gold. (201)

51b. Fools may be big, but great they can never be. (202)

52b. Not death is the result of loving. (216)

53b. All the world is bent on pleasure. (217)

54b. Honor for honor and love for love is due. (223)

55b. When the world tempts to sin any man who knows no law but his own, he will perish even among friends and kin. (233)

56b. One thing above all things precious is skill; add virtue and patience and you will do good to all your friends and to all your enemies, ill. (238)

57b. Importune not a man whose love you prize, for begging makes you hateful in his eyes. (253)

58b. A skilled hand, a well-trained elephant and a black rain-cloud give you what you want. (262)

59b. A man should flee from women when he knows what kind they are; whom they serve for gold or desire, they burn him up like fuel in a fire. (263)

60b. Your voice should always be gentle and sweet. (269)

61b. Shame upon him who wins gain or glory by the destruction of others. (287)

62b. If seed upon the rock you sow, though rain should come, it will not grow. (299)

63b. Boons to the unworthy are spent in vain; but the smallest favor to the good brings gain. (302)

64b. When joy turns to sorrow and weal to woe, patient souls will wring pleasure even from pain. (303)

65b. There is no act of sin that in this world may lie hidden; that which the fool considers secret even the spirits in woods know. (305)

66b. A world without friends is like a wilderness. (315)

67b. Weep for the living rather than for the dead. (317)

68b. The wife who shares in weal and woe, equal to either part, is fit to be the mate even of the king. (320)

69b. Neither deadly poison nor sharp-whetted sword is half as fatal as the ill-spoken word. (331)

70b. He who knows the measure of his own power and shows discretion in his speech, lives true to his duty and will triumph over his foes. (335)

71b. He who hurries when he should rest, and rests when he should hurry, destroys the tender fabric of his weal. (345)

72b. Anger in a wise man is never justified. (351)

73b. As children cry in vain to grasp the moon, so mortals idly mourn the dead. (354)

74b. A beast that speaks with the voice of man I have never seen. (359)

75b. There is no good, however slight, that man can gain from groans and mourning. (368)

76b. From four to eight, from thence to sixteen, and so on to thirty-two, insatiated greed goes on and on. (369)

77b. Another's faults are plainly seen; it is hard to see one's own. (374)

78b. When the earth appears to you as but an insignificant square, turn back, my son, and attempt no higher flight. (381)

79b. The man whom folly drives, his friends despise. (382)

80b. Men should meet death not with sadness, but as midmonth's festal joy. (388)

81b. When a man is free from evil stains, a sin the size of a hair-tip shows on him like a dark cloud. (392)

82b. No joy have mothers in a son whose comrades are no good. (397)

83b. First establish yourself in propriety, then teach. (400)

84b. A strong fool is not a good guard for the herd. (404)

85b. Brahmin, do you know in whose lonely heart much bitter sorrow lies? (413)

86b. Little desire is not enough; and much, brings much pain. (421)

87b. He who endures in troubled times is strong to reach the final bliss when trouble ends. (422)

88b. Blinding passions yield bitter fruit. (431)

89b. Righteousness protects the righteous like a cover in time of rain. (447)

90b. He to all creatures is kindly, against him no hatred is found. (451)

91b. Take not for best or for worst what first you hear. (466)

92b. Lust is the hook. (472)

93b. When entertained by another with food and drink, eat not too much, drink not too much. (477)

94b. A hundred thousand ditties all sung wrong are not worth one good one. (481)

95b. For this is true, I know it well—death will not pass me by. (497)

96b. A loving wife is ever hard to find, as is a man who to his wife is ever kind. (519)

97b. If wise, the wise and learned we would cultivate. (525)

98b. A woman dressed in smart clothes, standing before her door to stare about with idle gaze, soon from the path of virtue strays. (536)

99b. Of whom shall I be afraid, when I have done him no evil in thought, word, and deed, whereby I could come to misfortune? (545)

100b. A father's or a mother's or a sister's grief to lessen, a man should never hesitate even at the risk of his life. (547)

The Sayings of

CHRISTIANITY

A new commandment I
give to you, that you love
one another.

(John 13:34)

CHRISTIANITY

The term "Christian" was first applied to the followers of Jesus (as recorded in Acts 11:26) in the city of Antioch, in Syria. At that time the Christians were all Jews who considered themselves the True Israel, the Faithful Remnant, and the People of God who properly interpreted the Law and the Prophets. They did not consider themselves the followers of a new religion but the true interpreters of established Judaism. Their sacred scriptures were the Hebrew scriptures, and they fully accepted its teachings and its laws. They differed at first from the established orthodoxy in placing greater stress and value on repentance, on love of one's neighbor and on the hope of redemption. But their major difference was in their acceptance of the belief that Jesus of Nazareth was the Messiah, the *Christos,* foretold in the prophets.

As the teachings of Jesus incurred the enmity of the traditionalists, his followers were only strengthened in their belief and devotion, and they made central in their creed the acceptance of Jesus as the Christ, and that redemption was possible only through the acceptance of Jesus as the Son of God.

After the crucifixion of Jesus, his disciples gradually admitted to their ranks, regardless of race or language, all those who accepted Jesus as the Messiah. The Hebrew scriptures still remained their sacred books, but they used the Greek translation in their services, and not the Hebrew text; and they supplemented it in their sermons with stories, parables and sayings attributed to Jesus, which

45

demonstrated their teachings. Later they also used letters from missionary apostles to strengthen each other's faith and courage, or read inspirational or apocalyptic commentaries by the evangelists. And most of these materials were soon recorded.

Within two centuries a number of books appeared in different parts of the world, dealing with a variety of church problems, and giving the story of the life of Jesus as remembered by his contemporaries. The stories of the life of Jesus were called Gospels; and there is evidence that quite a number of Gospels existed at a very early time, of which only fragments are now extant. Toward the middle of the fourth century A.D., a number of these books were gathered together, and from them twenty-seven were selected as divinely inspired, and became the canon. The Christians by this time consisted mostly of gentiles and recognized themselves as followers of a religion distinct from Judaism. They retained the Hebrew scriptures, but called them the Old Testament. And to these they added the twenty-seven newly canonized books, called the New Testament.

Although a controversy arose at first about seven books included in the canon (Hebrews, James, 2 Peter, 2 and 3 John, Jude and Revelation), after a century or so the controversy died down, only to flare up again during the Reformation, when the inclusion of James was again questioned by Luther and others. But the canon remained unchanged; and it stands today as when it was first accepted by the Christian churches.

Christianity, which began as a reform movement within Judaism, soon threw off the racial and geographic nationalism of the older religion, and its evangelists labored to make it the religion of mankind. Today, Christianity is the most universally accepted of all the living religions, crosses the frontiers of almost every nation on earth, is known in every language and embraces all races. Every fourth person in the world is a Christian. In Europe and in the Americas Christianity is the dominant religion.

In the course of time, and for a diversity of reasons, a number of sectarian differences arose among the Christians, and today there are nearly 250 different sects, professing differences in creed, or differing in the interpretation of the creed. But all accept as fundamental the New Testament, which consists of four stories of the life of Jesus, known as the Gospels, the history of the apostolic missionary activities, known as The Acts, twenty-one missionary letters, known as The Epistles, and the apocalyptic Revelation. The essence of the wisdom and teachings of Christianity are to be found essentially in the Parables, as given in the first three Gospels; the sayings of Jesus and the Apostles, distributed throughout the New Testament, and the sayings of Jesus in apocryphal sources.

The Parables in the
GOSPELS

The parable, which means "comparison," is a distinct literary form which presents an actual or highly probable event of ordinary occurrence, in an extended simile, that leads to a higher, often religious, conclusion. The parable was used in the religious oral teaching of many religions, particularly among the Jews of biblical and postbiblical times. In the Old Testament we find "The Parable of the Bramble that Would Be King" in Judges 9:7-15; "The Parable of the Ewe Lamb" in II Samuel 12:1-4; "The Parable of the Prisoner" in I Kings 2:39-40; "The Parable of the Vineyard" in Isaiah 5:1-6; and "The Parable of the Two Eagles" in Ezekiel 13:2-10. And there are numerous parables in the Talmud.

The parable, as used in the teachings of Jesus, reached its classic literary form. The lofty moral was arrived at with the greatest economy of words, and the event was portrayed in stark realism. As a group, these parables vividly depict and faithfully portray the life in Palestine of their time where, for the most part, poor people tended small flocks of sheep, or cultivated small vineyards or went out to fish; some married, and many sorrowed in illness or bereavement; and young men longed for adventure in distant lands. There were a few rich men among them; and the people sometimes talked about a king who lived in a palace far away. The characters, in most of the parables, though barely suggested, come to life as if presented and developed in great detail. Some of the parables, such as "The Prodigal Son" and "The

Good Samaritan" and "The Rich Man and Lazarus," have a memorable completeness, brief as they are. Though many of the parables deal with comparisons as to what "the kingdom of heaven might be likened to," as a group they cover almost all the basic teachings of Christianity. In them we find the lesson, allegorically, of the importance of sowing good seed on good soil; how to approach new things and old; hypocrisy and sincerity as examplified by the "Two Men Who Prayed"; the greatness of compassion and service in "The Good Samaritan"; and the warning lesson for men who come unprepared to the King's Wedding. And each parable, lucidly and aptly, gives the perfect "comparison."

The number of parables have been variously given, from thirty to fifty-three, depending upon whether some similes (as given in the sayings of the New Testament) are included among the parables. Here thirty-six parables are given in the order of their appearance in the Gospels, and they present highlights of the teachings of Jesus. Only one parable was omitted (Luke, 16:1-9) because scholars agree that it is confusing in its implications.

The Parables of
JESUS

(In the order of their appearance in the Gospels)

1. A HOUSE BUILT ON SAND

Whoever hears these sayings of mine, and does them,
I will liken him to a wise man who built his house
upon a rock; and the rain descended, and the floods
came, and the winds blew and beat upon the house,
and it fell not; for it was founded upon a rock. But
every one who hears these sayings of mine, and does
them not, shall be likened to a foolish man who built
his house upon the sand; and the rain descended, and
the floods came, and the winds blew and beat upon
the house, and it fell; and great was the fall of it.
(Matt. 7:24-27) (Luke 6:46-49)

2. THE WEDDING GUEST

Then the disciples of John came to him, saying, "Why
do we and the Pharisees fast often, but your disciples
fast not?" And Jesus said to them, "Can the wedding
guests mourn as long as the bridegroom is with them?
But the day will come when the bridegroom will be
taken from them, and then they will fast." (Matt.
9:14-18) (Mark 2:18-20) (Luke 5:33-35)

3. NEW PATCHES FOR OLD TEARS

No one sews a piece of new cloth on an old garment,
for that which is put on to fill it up tears away from

the garment, and the tear is made worse. (Matt. 9:16) (Mark 2:2) (Luke 9:16)

4. NEW WINE IN OLD BOTTLES

Neither do men put new wine into old bottles; else the bottles might break and the wine run out and the bottles perish; but they put new wine into new bottles and both are preserved. (Matt. 9:17) (Mark 2:22) (Luke 5:37)

5. THE CHILDREN IN THE BAZAARS

To what shall I liken this generation? It is like children sitting in the bazaars and calling to their fellows, "We piped to you, and you did not dance; we mourned, and you did not lament." For John came neither eating nor drinking, and they say, "He has a devil." The Son of man came eating and drinking, and they say, "Behold, a man gluttonous and a winebibber, a friend of the publicans and sinners." Yet wisdom is justified by her deeds. (Matt. 11:16-19) (Luke 7:31-35)

6. THE PARABLE OF THE SOWER

Behold, a sower went out to sow. And as he sowed some seeds fell by the wayside, and the birds came and devoured them. Some fell upon stony places where they had not much earth, and forthwith they sprang up, but because they had no deepness of earth, when the sun rose they were scorched, and because they had no root, they withered away. And some seeds fell among thorns, and the thorns sprang up and choked them. But other seeds fell into good ground and brought forth fruit, some a hundredfold, some sixtyfold, some thirtyfold. (Matt. 13:3-8) (Mark 4:2-8) (Luke 8:4-6)

7. THE TARES AND THE WHEAT

The kingdom of heaven might be likened to a man who sowed good seed in his field; but while his men slept, an enemy came and sowed tares among the wheat, and went away. When the plants sprang up and brought forth grain, the tares appeared also. So the servants of the householder came and said to him, "Sir, did you not sow good seed in your field? From whence then has it tares?" He said to them, "An enemy has done this." The servants said to him, "Shall we go and gather them up?" But he said, "No, lest while you gather up the tares, you root up the wheat with them. Let both grow together until the harvest; and at that time I will say to the reapers, 'Gather first the tares and bind them in bundles to burn them, but gather the wheat into my barns.'" (Matt. 13:24-30, 36-43)

8. THE PARABLE OF THE MUSTARD SEED

The kingdom of heaven might be likened to a grain of mustard seed which a man took and sowed in his field; which is the least of all seeds, but when it has grown, it is the greatest among the herbs and becomes a tree, so that the birds of the air come and lodge in its branches. (Matt. 13:31-32) (Mark 4:30-32) (Luke 8:10-19)

9. THE PARABLE OF THE LEAVEN

The kingdom of heaven might be likened to leaven which a woman took and hid in three measures of flour, until the whole was leavened. (Matt. 13:33) (Luke 8:20-22)

10. THE HIDDEN TREASURE
Again, the kingdom of heaven might be likened to a treasure hidden in a field, which, when a man has found it he hides, and overjoyed goes and sells all that he has, and buys that field. (Matt. 13:44)

11. THE PEARL OF GREAT PRICE
The kingdom of heaven might be likened to a merchant seeking goodly pearls; who, when he found one pearl of great price, went and sold all that he had and bought it. (Matt. 13:45-46)

12. THE PARABLE OF THE DRAGNET
Again, the kingdom of heaven might be likened to a net that was cast into the sea and gathered fish of every kind; and when it was full, they drew it ashore and sat down and gathered the good into vessels, but cast away the bad. (Matt. 13:47-48)

13. NEW AND OLD TREASURES
Jesus said to them, "Have you understood all these things?" They answered him, "Yes, Lord." Then he said to them, "Then remember that every scribe who has been instructed in the kingdom of heaven is like a householder who brings forth out of his treasure things new and old." (Matt. 13:51-52)

14. THE LOST SHEEP
If a man has a hundred sheep, and one of them has gone astray, does he not leave the ninety-nine and

go into the mountains to seek the one that has strayed? And if he finds it, verily I say to you, he rejoices more over that sheep than over the ninety-nine which did not go astray. Even so, it is not the will of your Father who is in heaven that one of these little ones should perish. (Matt. 18:12-14) (Luke 15:3-7)

15. THE UNJUST STEWARD

The kingdom of heaven might be likened to a certain king who wished to settle accounts with his servants. When he began to reckon, one steward was brought to him who owed him ten thousand talents. But as he could not pay, his lord commanded him to be sold, with his wife and his children and all that he had, and payment to be made. The steward therefore fell down and worshipped him, saying, "Lord, have patience with me and I will repay you all." Then the king was moved with compassion and released him, and forgave him his debt.

But the same steward went out and found one of his fellow-servants who owed him a hundred *denarii,* and he laid hands on him and took him by the throat, saying, "Pay me what you owe!" His fellow-servant fell down at his feet and implored him, saying, "Have patience with me and I will repay you all." The steward would not, but went and cast him into prison until he should pay his debt. So when his fellow-servants saw what had been done, they were very sorry, and came and told the king all that had happened. Then the king called the steward and said to him, "O you wicked servant! I forgave you all that debt because you besought me. Should not you also have had compassion on your servant, even as I had pity on you?" And the king was angry and delivered him to the tormentors, till he should pay all that was due from him.

So likewise will my heavenly Father do also to you, if you from your hearts forgive not every one his brother their trespasses. (Matt. 18:23-35)

16. THE LABORERS IN THE VINEYARD

The kingdom of heaven might be likened to a householder who went out early in the morning to hire laborers for his vineyard. And when he had agreed with the laborers for a *dinarius* a day, he sent them into his vineyard. About the third hour he went out and saw others standing idle in the marketplace. And he said to them, "Go you also into the vineyard, and whatever is right I will pay you." And they went their way. He went out again about the sixth and the ninth hour and did likewise. And about the eleventh hour he went out and found still others standing idle, and said to them, "Why do you stand here idle all day?" They answered, "Because no man has hired us." He said to them, "Go you also into my vineyard; and whatever is right, that shall you receive."

When evening came, the owner of the vineyard said to his steward, "Call the laborers and give them their wage, beginning with the last and up to the first." And when these came who were hired about the eleventh hour, each man received a *dinarius*. But when the first came, they supposed that they would receive more; but they likewise received each a *dinarius*. And when they received it, they grumbled against him, saying, "These last worked but one hour, and you have made them equal to us who have borne the burden and heat of the day." But he answered one of them, and said, "Friend, I do you no wrong. Did you not agree with me to work for a *dinarius?* Take what is yours and go your way. I will give to the last, even as to you. Is it not lawful for me to do what I will with my own? Is your eye evil because I am good?"

So the last shall be first, and the first last. (Matt. 20:1-16)

17. THE TEST OF DEEDS

A certain man had two sons; and he came to the first, and said, "Son, go to work today in the vineyard." He answered, "I will not." But afterwards he repented and went. And he came to the second, and said likewise. And the son answered, "I will go, Sir," but he went not.

Jesus asked, "Now which of the two did the will of the father?"

They said to him, "The first."

Jesus said to them, "Verily I say to you that the publicans and the harlots go into the kingdom of heaven before you. For John came to you in the way of righteousness, and you believed him not; but the publicans and the harlots believed him. And you, when you had seen it, did not repent that you might believe him." (Matt. 21:28-32)

18. THE UNFAITHFUL TENANTS

There was a certain householder who planted a vineyard and hedged it in, and dug a winepress in it, and built a watch-tower, then let it out to tenants, and went away to a far country. And when the time of the vintage drew near, he sent his servants to the tenants for his share of the fruit. And the tenants took his servants, and beat one, and killed another, and stoned another. Again he sent other servants, more than the first time; and they did to them likewise. Last of all he sent to them his son, saying, "They will reverence my son." But when the tenants saw the son, they said to themselves, "This is the heir; come, let us kill him, and let us seize his inheritance." And they caught him and cast him out of the vineyard, and slew him.

Jesus asked, "When therefore the master of the vineyard comes, what will he do to those tenants?"

His disciples said to him, "He will miserably destroy those wicked men and let out his vineyard to other tenants who will render him his share of the fruit in their season."

Jesus said to them, "Did you never read in the Scriptures, 'The stone which the builders rejected, the same has become the cornerstone; this is the Lord's doing, and it is marvelous in our eyes.' Therefore I say to you, the kingdom of God will be taken from you and given to a nation that will produce the fruits of it. And whoever falls on this stone will be broken, and on whoever it falls it will grind him to powder." (Matt. 21:33-45) (Mark 12:1-11) (Luke 20:9-18)

19. THE MARRIAGE OF THE KING'S SON

The kingdom of heaven might be likened to a certain king who prepared a wedding-feast for his son. And he sent forth his servants to call those who were bidden to the wedding; but they would not come. Again he sent forth other servants, saying, "Tell those who are bidden, 'Behold, I have prepared the feast; my oxen and my fatlings are killed, and all things are ready; come to the wedding.'" But they made light of it and went their way, one to his farm, another to his merchandise; and the remainder took the king's servants and treated them spitefully, and slew them.

When the king heard of it he became angry and sent forth his troops and destroyed the murderers and burned their city. Then he said to his servants, "The wedding-feast is ready, but those who were bidden were not worthy. Go out, therefore, on the highways and invite as many as you shall find to the wedding." So the servants went out on the highways and gathered together as many as they found, both bad and good; and the wedding was furnished with guests.

And when the king came in to see the guests, he saw there a man who wore no wedding garment. And he said to him, "Friend, how came you here without a wedding garment?" And the man was speechless. Then said the king to his servants, "Bind him hand and foot and take him away, and cast him into outer darkness, there to weep and gnash his teeth."

For many are called, but few are chosen. (Matt. 22:2-14)

20. THE TEN VIRGINS

When the kingdom of heaven might be likened to ten virgins who took their lamps and went out to meet the bridegroom. Five of them were wise, and five were foolish. The foolish ones took their lamps, but took no oil with them. But the wise took oil in their vessels with their lamps. While the bridegroom tarried, they all slumbered and slept. And at midnight there was a cry, "Behold, the bridegroom is coming; go out to meet him!"

Then all the virgins arose and trimmed their lamps. And the foolish said to the wise, "Give us of your oil, for our lamps have gone out." But the wise answered, "There might not be enough for both us and you; go rather to those who sell, and buy oil for yourselves." And while they went to buy oil, the bridegroom came, and those who were ready went in with him to the wedding-feast, and the door was shut. Afterward the other virgins came, saying, "Lord! Lord! Open the door to us!" But he answered, "Verily, I say to you, I know you not."

Watch therefore, for you know not the day nor the hour when the Son of man comes. (Matt. 25:1-13)

21. THE TALENTS AND THE POUNDS

The kingdom of heaven might be likened to a man who, before travelling to a far country, called his servants and entrusted them with his goods. To one he gave five talents, to another two, and to another one; to each man according to his ability; and at once went on his journey. Then he who had received the five talents went and traded with the same and made five talents more. Likewise he who had received two talents he also gained two more. But he who had received one went and dug in the earth, and hid his master's money.

After a long time the master returned and settled accounts with those servants. And so he who had received five talents came and brought five more talents, saying, "Lord, you delivered to me five talents; behold, I have gained besides them five talents more." His master said to him, "Well done, good and faithful servant. You have been faithful over a few things; I will make you ruler over many things. Enter into the joy of your master."

He also who had received two talents came and said, "Lord, you delivered to me two talents; behold, I have gained two talents besides them." His master said to him, "Well done, good and faithful servant. You have been faithful over a few things; I will make you ruler over many things. Enter into the joy of your master."

Then he who had received the one talent came and said, "Lord, I knew that you are a hard man, reaping where you have not sown, and gathering where you have not winnowed. So I was afraid, and went and hid your talent in the earth. Lo, here is what is yours." His master answered, "You wicked and slothful servant. You knew that I reap where I have not sown, and gather where I have not winnowed. You ought therefore to have put my money where at my coming I should have received my own with interest."

"Therefore take the talent away from him and give it to him who has the ten. For to everyone who has shall be given, and he shall have abundance; but from him who has not shall be taken away even that which he has." And he cast the unprofitable servant

into outer darkness there to weep and gnash his
teeth. (Matt. 25:14-30) (Luke 19:12-28)

22. THE LAST JUDGMENT

When the Son of man comes in his glory, and all the
holy angels with him, then he will sit upon the throne
of his glory. And before him will be gathered all nations; and he will separate them one from another,
as a shepherd separates his sheep from the goats.
And he will set the sheep at his right hand, but
the goats will be at the left.

Then will the King say to those at his right hand,
"Come, you whom my Father has blessed, inherit
the kingdom prepared for you from the foundation
of the world. For when I was hungry, you gave me
food; and when I was thirsty, you gave me drink;
when I was a stranger, you took me in; when naked,
you clothed me; when I was sick, you visited me; and
when I was in prison, you came to me."

Then the righteous will answer him, saying,
"Lord, when did we see you hungry and fed you; or
thirsty, and gave you drink? When did we see you a
stranger and took you in; or naked, and clothed you?
When did we see you sick, or in prison, and came to
you?"

And the King will answer, "Verily I say to you,
inasmuch as you have done to one of the least of my
brothers, you have done it to me."

Then will he say to those at his left hand, "Depart from me, you accursed, into everlasting fire prepared for the devil and his angels! For when I was
hungry, you gave me no food, and when I was thirsty,
you gave me no drink; when I was a stranger, you

did not take me in; when I was naked, you clothed me not; sick and in prison, and you visited me not."

Then will they also answer him, saying, "Lord, when did we see you hungry, or thirsty, or a stranger, or naked, or sick, or in prison, and did not minister to you?"

And he will answer them, saying, "Verily I say to you, inasmuch as you did not do it to the least of my brothers, you did not do it to me."

And these will go away into everlasting punishment; but the righteous, to life eternal. (Matt. 25:31-46)

23. THOSE WHO NEED THE PHYSICIAN

As Jesus sat at table in his house, many publicans and sinners sat also with Jesus and his disciples, for there were many among his followers. And when the scribes and Pharisees saw him eat with publicans and sinners, they said to his disciples, "How is it that he eats and drinks with publicans and sinners?"

When Jesus heard this, he said to them, "They who are well have no need of the physician, but they who are sick. I came not to call the righteous, but sinners to repentance." (Mark 2:15-17)

24. THE GROWING SEED

The kingdom of God might be likened to a man who scattered seed upon the ground; and then sleeps at night and rises each day, and the seed springs up and grows, he knows not how. For the earth brings forth fruit of itself; first the blade, then the ear, and after that the full grain in the ear. But as soon as the grain has ripened, immediately he puts in the sickle, because the harvest has come. (Mark 4:26-29)

25. THE TWO DEBTORS

One of the Pharisees asked Jesus to eat with him. And he went to the Pharisee's house and sat down at the table. And behold, a woman in the city who was a sinner, when she heard that Jesus sat down to eat in the Pharisee's house, brought an alabaster box of ointment, and stood at his feet weeping, and began to wash his feet with tears, and wiped them with the hair of her head, and kissed his feet, and anointed them with the ointment.

When the Pharisee who had invited him saw it, he said to himself, "This man, if he were really a prophet, would have known who and what manner of woman this is who touches him, for she is a sinner."

And Jesus said to him, "Simon, I have something to say to you."

And the Pharisee said, "Master, say on."

"There was a certain creditor who had two debtors; one owed him five hundred *denarii*, and the other, fifty. And when they could not repay him, he frankly forgave them both. Tell me, which of them will love him most?"

Simon answered, "I suppose that he to whom he forgave most."

And he said to him, "You have judged rightly." And he turned to the woman and said to Simon, "Do you see this woman? I entered your house and you gave me no water for my feet; but she has washed my feet with tears and wiped them with the hair of her head. You gave me no kiss, but this woman, since the time I came in, has not ceased to kiss my feet. You did not anoint my head with ointment, but this woman has anointed my feet with ointment. Therefore, I say to you, her sins, which are many, are forgiven, for she loved much; but to whom little is forgiven, the same loves little."

And he said to her, "Your sins are forgiven."

The men who sat at table with him began to say to themselves, "Who is this who forgives sins also?"

And Jesus said to the woman, "Your faith has saved you; go in peace." (Luke 7:36-50)

26. THE GOOD SAMARITAN

A certain lawyer stood up to test Jesus, saying, "Master, what must I do to inherit eternal life?" Jesus said to him, "What is written in the Law?"

He answered, " 'You shall love the Lord your God with all your heart and with all your soul and with all your strength and with all your mind; and you shall love your neighbor as yourself.' "

Jesus said to him, "You have answered right. This do and you shall live."

But he, wishing to justify his question, said to Jesus, "And who is my neighbor?"

And Jesus answered, "A certain man went down from Jerusalem to Jericho, and fell among thieves who stripped him of his garments and wounded him, and departed, leaving him half dead. By chance a certain priest came down that way; and when he saw him, he passed by on the other side. And likewise a Levite, when he came to that place, saw and looked at him and passed by on the other side. But a certain Samaritan, as he journeyed, came to where the man was and when he saw him, had compassion on him, and went to him and dressed his wounds with oil and wine, and set him on his own beast, and brought him to an inn, and took care of him. On the morrow before he departed, he took out two *denarii* and gave them to the innkeeper and said, 'Take care of him; and whatever you spend more, when I come again I will repay you.' Which of these three think you, was neighbor to him who fell among the thieves?"

And he said, "He who showed mercy on him."

Then said Jesus to him, "Go and do likewise." (Luke 10:25-37)

27. FRIENDS AT MIDNIGHT

And Jesus said to them, "Which of you who has a friend, shall go to him at midnight, and say to him, 'Friend, lend me three loaves; for a friend of mine on his journey has come to me, and I have nothing to set before him,' and he from within shall answer, 'Trouble me not. The door is now shut, and my children are with me in bed. I cannot rise and give it to you.'

"I say to you, though he will not rise and give it to him because he is his friend, yet because of his importunity he will rise and give him as many loaves as he needs. And I say to you, ask, and it shall be given you; seek, and you shall find; knock, and it shall be opened to you.

"For every one who asks, receives; and he who seeks, finds; and to him who knocks it shall be opened.

"If a son shall ask bread of any of you who is a father, will he give him a stone? Or if he asks for a fish, will he for a fish give him a serpent? Or if he shall ask an egg, will he offer him a scorpion?

"If you then, being evil, know how to give good gifts to your children, how much more shall your heavenly Father give the Holy Spirit to those who ask him?" (Luke 11:5-13)

28. THE RICH FOOL

The ground of a certain rich man yielded plentifully. And he thought to himself, What shall I do, for I have no room where to store my crops? And he said, "This I will do: I will pull down my barns and build greater ones; and there I will store all my fruit and crops. And I will say to my Soul, 'Soul, you have great wealth stored up for many years. Take your ease; eat, drink, and be merry.'"

But God said to him, "O fool! This night your soul shall be required of you; then whose shall those things be which you have provided?"

So is he who lays up treasure for himself and is not rich toward God. (Luke 12:16-21)

29. THE BARREN FIG TREE

A certain man had a fig tree planted in his vineyard; and he came to look for fruit on it but could find none. Then he said to the dresser of his vineyard, "Behold, these three years I come seeking fruit on this fig tree and find none. Cut it down! Why should it encumber the ground?" And he answered, "Master, let it alone this year also. I shall dig about it and dung it, and if it bears fruit, well; and if not, then after that you shall cut it down." (Luke 13:6-9)

30. THE GREAT FEAST

A certain man made a great feast and invited many guests; and at supper-time he sent his servant to say to those who were invited, "Come, for all things are now ready." But they all with one accord began to make excuses. The first said, "I have bought a piece of land and must go to see it. I pray you, have me excused." Another said, "I have bought five yoke of oxen and must go to prove them. I pray you, have me excused." And another said, "I have married, and therefore I cannot come."

So the servant returned and reported to his master these things. Then the master of the house being angry said to his servant, "Go out quickly into the streets and lanes of the city and bring in here the poor, and the maimed, and the halt and the blind."

The servant returned and said, "Master, what you have commanded is done, and yet there is still room." The master said to the servant, "Go out on the highways and among the hedges, and compel them to come in so that my house may be filled. For I say to you that none of those who were invited shall taste of my supper." (Luke 14:16-24)

31. THE KING'S RASH WARFARE

What king, going to make war against another king, does not sit down first and consult whether he is able with ten thousand to meet him who comes against him with twenty thousand?

Or else, while the other is yet a great way off, he sends an embassy to ask conditions of peace.

So likewise, whoever of you who forsakes not all

that he has, he cannot be my disciple. (Luke 14: 31-33)

32. THE LOST COIN

What woman having ten pieces of silver, if she loses one piece, does not light a candle, and sweep the house and search diligently until she finds it? And when she has found it, she calls her friends and her neighbors together, saying, "Rejoice with me, for I have found the piece which I had lost."

Likewise, I say to you, there is joy in the presence of the angels of God over one sinner who repents. (Luke 15:8-10)

33. THE PRODIGAL SON

A certain man had two sons; and the younger of them said to his father, "Father, give me my portion of the property that falls to me." And he divided his property between them. Not many days afterwards, the younger son gathered together all he had and journeyed to a far country, and there wasted his substance in riotous living.

And when he had spent all he had, there arose a mighty famine in that land, and he began to be in want. He went and joined himself to a citizen of that country who sent him into his fields to feed swine. And he would have gladly filled his belly with the husks the swine ate, but no one gave them to him. When he came to himself, he said, "How many of my father's servants have bread enough and to spare while I perish with hunger! I will arise and go to my father, and will say to him, 'Father, I have sinned against heaven, and before you, and am no more worthy to be called your son; but treat me as one of your hired servants.' "

He arose and went to his father. But while he was a great way off, his father saw him and had compassion, and ran and fell on his neck, and kissed him.

The son said, "Father, I have sinned against heaven and in your sight, and am no more worthy to be called your son."

But the father said to his servants, "Bring forth the best robe and put it on him. And put a ring on his hand and shoes on his feet. And bring the fatted calf and kill it; and let us eat and be merry. For this my son was dead, and now is alive again; he was lost, and is found."

So they began to be merry.

Now his elder son was in the field; and as he came home and drew nigh the house, he heard music and dancing. And he called one of the servants and asked what these things meant. The servant said to him, "Your brother has come, and your father has killed the fatted calf because he has returned safe and sound."

But the older brother was angry and would not go in. Therefore his father came out and entreated him. And he said to his father, "Lo, these many years I served you without at any time transgressing your command, and yet you never gave me a kid, that I might make merry with my friends. But as soon as this your son came, who has devoured your substance with harlots, you killed for him the fatted calf."

And the father said to him, "Son, you are ever with me, and all that I have is yours. But it was fitting that we should make merry and be glad. For this your brother was dead, and is alive again; he was lost, and now is found." (Luke 15:11-32)

34. THE RICH MAN AND LAZARUS

There was a certain rich man who was clothed in purple and fine linen, and fared sumptuously every day. And there was a certain beggar named Lazarus who was put down at his gate full of sores, and eager to be fed with the crumbs which fell from the rich man's table; moreover the dogs came and licked his sores.

And it came to pass that the beggar died and was carried by the angels to Abraham's bosom. The rich man also died and was buried; and in hell he lifted up his eyes, being in torment, and saw Abraham afar off and Lazarus with him. And he cried out, "Father Abraham, have mercy on me and send Lazarus that he may dip the tip of his finger in water and cool my tongue, for I am tormented in this flame!"

But Abraham said, "Son, remember that you in your lifetime received good things and Lazarus, evil things; but now he is comforted and you are tormented. And besides all this, between us and you there is a great gulf fixed, so that those who want to pass from here to you cannot; nor can they pass from your side to us."

Then he said, "I pray you, father, send him to my father's house. For I have five brothers; and let him testify to them, else they also would come to this place of torment."

Abraham said to him, "They have Moses and the prophets; let them listen to them."

And he said, "No, Father Abraham; but if one went to them from the dead they will repent."

And Abraham said to him, "If they hear not Moses and the prophets, neither will they be persuaded though one rose from the dead." (Luke 16: 19-31)

35. THE UNJUST JUDGE

There was in a city a judge who feared not God nor regarded men. And there was a widow in that city who came to him, saying, "Protect me from my adversary." He would not for a while; but afterwards he said to himself, "Though I fear not God nor regard man, yet because this widow troubles me, I will protect her, lest by her continual coming she may weary me."

And the Lord said, "Hear what the unjust judge has said. And shall not God protect his own elect who cry out to him day and night? I tell you he will protect them speedily. Nevertheless, when the Son of man comes, will he find faith on earth?" (Luke 18:2-8)

36. TWO MEN WHO PRAYED

Two men went up into the temple to pray; the one a Pharisee, and the other a publican. The Pharisee stood and prayed thus, "God, I thank you that I am not as other men are, extortionists, unjust, adulterers, or even as this publican. I fast twice a week; and I give tithes of all I possess."

And the publican, standing far off, would not as much as lift up his eyes to heaven, but smote his breast, saying, "O God, be merciful to me a sinner!"

I tell you, this man went down to his house justified rather than the other. For everyone who exalts himself will be abased; and he who humbles himself will be exalted. (Luke 18:10-14)

The Sayings of the
NEW TESTAMENT

1. Man shall not live by bread alone. (Matt. 4:4)

2. Blessed are the poor in spirit, for theirs is the kingdom of heaven. (Matt. 5:3)

3. Blessed are they who mourn, for they shall be comforted. (Matt. 5:4)

4. Blessed are the meek, for they shall inherit the earth. (Matt. 5:5)

5. Blessed are they who hunger and thirst after righteousness, for they shall be filled. (Matt. 5:6)

6. Blessed are the merciful, for they shall obtain mercy. (Matt. 5:7)

7. Blessed are the pure in heart, for they shall see God. (Matt. 5:8)

8. Blessed are the peacemakers, for they shall be called the children of God. (Matt. 5:9)

9. If the salt should lose its savor, how shall its saltiness be restored? It becomes good for nothing, but to be cast out and to be trodden underfoot. (Matt. 5:13)

10. Men do not light a candle and put it under a bushel, but on a candlestick; and it gives light to all who are in the house. (Matt. 5:15)

73

11. Whoever looks on a woman lustfully has already committed adultery with her in his heart. (Matt. 5:28)

12. Let your "yea" be "yea" and your "nay" be "nay." (Matt. 5:37)

13. Resist not evil; but whoever shall smite you on your right cheek, turn to him the other also. (Matt. 5:39)

14. Love your enemies, bless them who curse you, do good to them who hate you, and pray for them who spitefully use you and persecute you. (Matt. 5:44)

15. Your Father who is in heaven makes the sun rise on the evil and on the good, and sends rain on the just and on the unjust. (Matt. 5:45)

16. When you pray, do not use vain repetitions, for your Father knows what you are in need of before you ask him. (Matt. 6:7-8)

17. If you forgive not men their trespasses, neither will your Father forgive your trespasses. (Matt. 6:15)

18. Where your treasure is there will your heart be also. (Matt. 6:21)

19. If your eye is evil, your entire body will be full of darkness. (Matt. 6:23)

20. No man can serve two masters; for either he will hate the one and love the other, or else he will hold to the one and despise the other. You cannot serve God and Mammon. (Matt. 6:24)

21. Take no thought for your life, what you shall eat or what you shall drink; nor for your body, what you shall put on. Is not life more than food, and the body more than raiment? (Matt. 6:25)

22. Behold the birds of the air; for they sow not, neither do they reap, nor gather into barns, yet your heavenly Father feeds them. (Matt. 6:26)

23. Which of you by taking thought can add one cubit to his stature? (Matt. 6:27)

24. Consider the lilies of the field, how they grow. They toil not neither do they spin, yet even Solomon in all his glory was not arrayed like one of these. (Matt. 6:29)

25. Sufficient unto the day is the evil thereof. (Matt. 6:34)

26. Judge not, that you be not judged. (Matt. 7:1)

27. Why do you behold the speck in your brother's eye but do not consider the beam in your own eye? (Matt. 7:3)

28. Give not that which is holy to the dogs, neither cast your pearls before swine, lest they trample them underfoot and turn to rend you. (Matt. 7:6)

29. Ask, and it will be given to you; seek, and you will find; knock, and it will be opened to you. (Matt. 7:7)

30. What man is there who, when his son asks for bread, will give him a stone? (Matt. 7:9)

31. Whatever you would that men should do to you, do so to them; for this is the law of the prophets. (Matt. 7:12)

32. Wide is the gate and broad is the way that leads to destruction, and many there are who enter it; but narrow is the gate which leads to life, and few there are who find it. (Matt. 7:13-14)

33. Beware of false prophets who come to you in sheep's clothing but inwardly are ravenous wolves. (Matt. 7:15)

34. You will know them by their fruit. Do men gather grapes from thorn-bushes or figs from thistles? (Matt. 7:16)

35. A good tree cannot bring forth evil fruit; neither can a corrupt tree bring forth good fruit. (Matt. 7:18)

36. Let the dead bury their dead. (Matt. 8:22)

37. Those who are well need no physician, but those who are sick. (Matt. 9:12)

38. Be wise as serpents and harmless as doves. (Matt. 10:16)

39. He who endures to the end will be saved. (Matt. 10:22)

40. A house divided against itself will not stand. (Matt. 12:25)

41. He who is not with me is against me. (Matt. 12:30)

42. O generation of vipers, how can you, being evil, speak good things? (Matt. 12:24)

43. Out of the abundance of the heart the mouth speaks. (Matt. 12:34)

44. By your words you will be justified; and by your words you will be condemned. (Matt. 12:37)

45. Whoever does the will of my Father who is in heaven, the same is my brother, and sister, and mother. (Matt. 12:50)

46. A prophet is not without honor, except in his own country and in his own house. (Matt. 13:57)

47. Not that which goes into his mouth defiles a man, but that which comes out of it. (Matt. 15:11)

48. If the blind lead the blind, both shall fall into the ditch. (Matt. 16:14)

49. Whoever will save his life shall lose it; and whoever will lose his life for My sake shall find it. (Matt. 16:25)

50. What will it profit a man if he should gain the whole world, if he loses his own soul? (Matt. 16:26)

51. If you have faith as a grain of mustard-seed, you shall say to this mountain, "Move hence to yonder place," and it shall move; and nothing shall be impossible to you. (Matt. 17:20)

52. Woe to the world because of offenses! (Matt. 18:17)

53. If your brother trespasses against you, go and tell him his fault between you and him alone. (Matt. 18:15)

54. What God has joined together, let no man put asunder. (Matt. 19:6)

55. You shall love your neighbor as yourself. (Matt. 19:19)

56. It is easier for a camel to go through the eye of a needle, than for a rich man to enter into the kingdom of God. (Matt. 19:24)

57. With God all things are possible. (Matt. 19:26)

58. Out of the mouth of babes and sucklings you have perfected praise. (Matt. 21:16)

59. Whatever you ask for in prayer, believing, you will receive. (Matt. 21:22)

60. Many are called, but few are chosen. (Matt. 22:14)

61. Render to Caesar the things that are Caesar's; and to God, the things that are God's. (Matt. 22:21)

62. You shall love the Lord your God with all your heart and with all your soul and with all your mind. This is the first and great commandment. And the second is like it: You shall love your neighbor as yourself. On these two commandments rest all the Law and the prophets. (Matt. 22:37)

63. Whoever shall exalt himself shall be abased; and he that shall humble himself shall be exalted. (Matt. 23:12)

64. Woe to you, blind guides, who strain at a gnat and swallow a camel! (Matt. 23:25)

65. Where the carcass is, there will the vultures be gathered together. (Matt. 24:28)

66. Inasmuch as you have done it to the least of My brothers, you have done it to Me. (Matt. 25:40)

67. The spirit indeed is willing; but the flesh is weak. (Matt. 26:41)

68. The Sabbath was made for man and not man for the Sabbath. (Mark 2:27)

69. When you pray, forgive if you have anything against anyone, that your Father who is in heaven may forgive you your trespasses. (Mark 11:25)

70. Physician, heal yourself. (Luke 4:23)

71. No prophet is accepted in his own country. (Luke 4:24)

72. Love your enemies; do good to them who hate you. (Luke 6:27)

73. To him who smites you on one cheek offer also the other; and to him who takes away your cloak, do not withhold your coat also. (Luke 6:29)

74. As you would that men should do to you, do you also to them likewise. (Luke 6:31)

75. If you love those who love you, what thanks do you deserve? And if you do good to them who do good to you, what thanks do you deserve? For sinners do so also. (Luke 6:32-34)

76. Judge not, and you will not be judged; condemn not, and you will not be condemned; forgive, and you will be forgiven. (Luke 6:37)

77. With the measure that you mete out to others, it will be measured to you. (Luke 6:38)

78. Can the blind lead the blind? (Luke 6:39)

79. To whom little is forgiven, the same loves little. (Luke 7:47)

80. The laborer is worthy of his hire. (Luke 10:87)

81. He who is faithful in little is also faithful in much; and he who is dishonest in little is also dishonest in much. (Luke 16:10)

82. If your brother trespass against you seven times a day, and seven times a day turn to you and say, "I repent," you should forgive him. (Luke 17:3-4)

83. The kingdom of God is within you. (Luke 17:21)

84. The wind blows where it wills. (John 3:8)

85. He who is without sin among you, let him first cast a stone at her. (John 8:7)

86. A new commandment I give to you: That you love one another. (John 13:34)

87. In my Father's house are many mansions. (John 14:2)

88. Greater love has no man than this, that a man lay down his life for his friends. (John 15:13)

89. God is no respecter of persons. (Acts 10:34)

90. He has made of one blood all nations of men. (Acts 17:26)

91. It is more blessed to give than to receive. (Acts 20:35)

92. The just shall live by faith. (Romans 1:17)

93. Not the hearers of the law are just before God, but the doers of the law. (Romans 2:13)

94. The wages of sin are death. (Romans 6:23)

95. The good that I would do, I do not; but the evil which I would not, that I do. (Romans 7:19)

96. All things work together for good to those who love God. (Romans 8:28)

97. Has not the potter power over the clay, of the same lump to make one vessel to honor and another to dishonor? (Romans 9:21)

98. Be not wise in your own conceits. (Romans 12:16)

99. Recompense to no man evil for evil. (Romans 12:17)

100. As much as lies within your power, live peaceably with all men. (Romans 12:18)

101. If your enemy hungers, feed him; and if he thirsts,

give him drink; for in so doing you shall heap coals of fire on his head. (Romans 12:20)

102. None of us lives to himself; and no man dies to himself. (Romans 15:7)

103. There is nothing unclean in itself; but to him who esteems anything to be unclean, to him it is unclean. (Romans 14:14)

104. God has chosen the foolish things of the world with which to confound the wise; and he has chosen the weak things of the world with which to confound the mighty. (I Corin. 1:27)

105. A little leaven leavens the whole lump. (I Corin. 5:6)

106. It is better to marry than to burn. (I Corin. 7:9)

107. Those who run in the race are many, but one receives the prize. (I Corin. 9:24)

108. Let him who thinks he stands take heed lest he fall. (I Corin. 10:12)

109. Whatever you do, do all to the glory of God. (I Corin. 10:31)

110. Though I speak with the tongues of men and of angels, and have not charity I am as sounding brass, or a tinkling cymbal. And though I have the gift of prophecy and understand all mysteries and all knowledge; and though I have all faith, so that I could move mountains, and have not charity, I am nothing. (I Corin. 13:1-2)

111. Charity envies not; charity vaunts not itself, is not puffed up, is not easily provoked; thinks no evil; rejoices

not in iniquity, but rejoices in the truth; bears all things, believes all things, hopes all things, endures all things. (I Corin. 13:4)

112. When I was a child, I spoke as a child; but when I became a man I put away childish things. (I Corin. 13:11)

113. And now abide faith, hope, charity, these three; but the greatest of these is charity. (I Corin. 13:13)

114. If the trumpet gives an uncertain sound, who shall prepare himself for the battle? (I Corin. 14:18)

115. Let us eat and drink, for tomorrow we die. (I Corin. 15:32)

116. He who had gathered much had nothing over; and he who had gathered little had no lack. (II Corin. 8:15)

117. God loves a cheerful giver. (II Corin. 9:7)

118. You suffer fools gladly, since you consider yourselves wise. (II Corin. 11:19)

119. Every man shall bear his own burden. (Gal. 6:5)

120. Whatever a man sows, that shall he also reap. (Gal. 6:7)

121. There is one God and Father of all, who is above all, and through all, and in you all. (Ephes. 4:6)

122. Let not the sun go down upon your wrath. (Ephes. 4:26)

123. Let your moderation be known to all men. (Phil. 4:5)

124. I have learned, in whatever state I am in, with that to be content. (Phil. 4:11)

125. Let your speech always be with grace, seasoned with salt, that you may know how you ought to answer every man. (Col. 4:6)

126. Learn to be quiet and to attend to your own affairs, and to work with your own hands. (I Thes. 4:11)

127. See that no one renders evil for evil to any man. (I Thes. 5:15)

128. Follow that which is good, both among yourselves and to all men. (I Thes. 5:15)

129. If anyone does not work, neither should he eat. (II Thes. 3:10)

130. We brought nothing into this world, and it is certain we can carry nothing out. (I Tim. 6:7)

131. The love of money is the root of all evil. (I Tim. 6:10)

132. Speak evil of no man. (Titus 1:2)

133. To the pure all things are pure. (Titus 1:15)

134. Faith is the substance of things hoped for, the evidence of things not seen. (Heb. 11:1)

135. He who wavers is like a wave of the sea driven and tossed by the wind. (James 1:6)

136. A double-minded man is unstable in all his ways. (James 1:8)

137. Let no one say when he is tempted, "I am tempted by God." (James 1:13)

138. When lust has conceived, it brings forth sin; and when sin matures, it brings forth death. (James 1:15)

139. Let every man be swift to hear, slow to speak, slow to anger. (James 1:19)

140. Be doers of the word, and not hearers only. (James 1:22)

141. Pure religion before God is to visit the fatherless and widows in their affliction, and to keep oneself unspotted from the world. (James 1:27)

142. If you show partiality, you commit sin. (James 2:9)

143. So speak and so do as those who shall be judged by the law of liberty. (James 2:12)

144. Of what profit a man who says he has faith, but has not good works? Can faith save him? (James 2:14)

145. By works a man is justified, and not by faith alone. (James 2:24)

146. As the body without the spirit is dead, so also faith without good works is dead. (James 2:26)

147. Behold the ships which, though they are so great and driven by fierce winds, yet are turned about with a very small rudder at the will of the pilot. (James 3:4)

148. How great a conflagration a little fire kindles! (James 3:5)

149. The tongue no man can tame; it is an unruly devil. (James 3:8)

150. Out of the same mouth come blessings and curses. (James 3:10)

151. The fruit of righteousness is sown in peace by peace-makers. (James 3:18)

152. He who speaks evil of his brother and judges him, speaks evil of the Law and judges it. (James 4:11)

153. Who are you that you judge another? (James 4:12)

154. What is your life? It is a vapor that appears for a little time and then vanishes away. (James 4:14)

155. He who knows what is right and does it not, to him it is sin. (James 4:17)

156. Confess your faults one to another, and pray one for another, that you may be healed. (James 5:16)

157. God resists the proud and gives grace to the humble. (I Peter 5:5)

158. God is light, and in him is no darkness at all. (I John 1:5)

159. If we say we are without sin, we deceive ourselves, and the truth is not in us. (I John 1:8)

160. God is love; and he who dwells in love dwells in God. (I John 4:16)

161. There is no fear in love; but perfect love casts out fear. (I John 4:18)

162. If a man says, "I love God," but hates his brother, he is a liar. (I John 4:21)

163. He who loves God loves his brother also. (I John 4:21)

164. Every man shall be judged according to his work. (Rev. 20:13)

The
AGRAPHA *and the* LOGIA

Agrapha, in Greek, means unwritten, and the word is used to describe a number of sayings attributed to Jesus which, though not found in the canonical Gospels, were current in early oral Christian tradition and found their way into apocryphal works. Examples are found in the New Testament itself, as when St. Paul quotes Jesus, "It is more blessed to give than to receive" (Acts 20:35), a saying not found in the Gospels; and other sayings are quoted or given in noncanonical Christian works.

Not until the end of the seventeenth century were attempts made to gather together these extracanonical sayings. In 1859 a German scholar, Lobegott F. C. von Tischendorf, discovered the Codex Sinaiticus of the Greek Bible in the Convent of St. Catherine at the foot of Mount Sinai, and it contained a few hitherto unauthenticated sayings. And about two decades later, two British archeologists, Drs. Grenfell and Hunt, who were digging in Upper Egypt, West of the Nile, where the capitol of Oxyrhynchus Province had once stood, found a vast quantity of papyri, chiefly Greek, ranging from the first to the eighth century. Among the papyri was a leaf, belonging somewhere between 150 and 300 A.D., on which was written a group of sayings.

These, together with the sayings in the Tischendorf Bible, and in other fragments of lost Bibles recently discovered, were named *Logia*.

The following thirty-four *Logia* are taken from the Oxyrhynchus papyri and from fragments of other documents. Some of these fragments, as found, are so mutilated that often nearly half of a saying must be supplied from the implication of the available or readable half. Here they are given without the impediments of question marks for words difficult to decipher, and dots for words missing.

Sayings from the
AGRAPHA *and the* LOGIA

1a. I am thou, and thou art I, and where thou art there am I also; and in all things am I sown. And from whence-soever thou gatherest me, in gathering me thou gatherest thyself.

2a. He who seeks will find; and finding, will wonder; and wondering, will reign; and reigning, will rest.

3a. The soul must be made to grow through faith and knowledge.

4a. Kind words are better than ointment, and a sweet saying than the perfume of love.

5a. A cheerful countenance is as the appearance of sweetness.

6a. Love rules willing hearts; fear, the unwilling.

7a. The giver is happier than the receiver.

8a. Never be joyful, except when you have seen your brother in love.

9a. Love covers a multitude of sins.

10a. You see your brother; you see your God.

11a. There are those who stretch the warps and weave nothing.

12a. Blessed is he who also fasts for this, that he might feed the poor.

13a. You have dismissed the living, who were before you, and talk of the dead.

14a. When you fast, pray for those who are about to perish.

15a. A man not tempted is not proved.

16a. Anger destroys even the prudent.

17a. Where there are pains, thither runs the physician.

18a. Excepting for a few saints, men have always thought that they could atone for their crimes with money.

19a. You hear with one ear, but the other you have closed.

20a. If anyone does not work, let not such a one eat; for the Lord our God hates the slothful.

21a. The Heavenly Father desires rather the repentance than the punishment of sinners.

22a. The world shall be built up through grace.

23a. Show yourself a tried money-changer, in that you can distinguish between good and bad coin.

24a. Ask great things, and the small shall be added; ask heavenly things, and the earthly shall be added.

25a. He to who more is forgiven, loves more.

26a. No one shall be called good who mixes evil with the good, for gall does not mix well with honey.

27a. Men must give an account of every good word that they fail to speak.

28a. If you cannot keep that which is small, who will entrust you with that which is great? For he that is faithful in very little, is also faithful in much.

29a. As you judge, so shall you be judged.

30a. Blessed are they who mourn the destruction of the unbelievers.

31a. Let us resist all iniquity and hold it in hatred,

32a. Beware how you sit with sinners.

33a. Take not the world for your lord; lest it take you for its slave.

34a. One day Jesus and his disciples passed a man who spoke evil of them in a loud voice; but Jesus spoke only good in return. And when his disciples asked him why he spoke good to him who spoke evil, he replied: "Each gives out of his store."

The Sayings of

CONFUCIANISM

Confucius was asked: "Is there one word
that sums up the basis of all good conduct?"
And he replied, "Is not 'reciprocity'
that word? What you yourself do
not desire, do not put before
others." (*Analects*, XV)

CONFUCIANISM

Confucius was born in 551 B.C. and lived to the age of seventy-two. As a young man he met the founder of Taoism, who was by then an old man, but the mysticism of the Old Philosopher struck no sympathetic chord in the young classicist. Confucius, after holding several public offices, withdrew to devote himself to editing the Chinese classics and interpreting them.

The ancient classics which Confucius resurrected, refurbished and preserved in the new form he gave them, in time became the Confucian Holy Scriptures; and they are known as the *Five King* or the Five Ancient Classics. Actually, not all five were ancient in his day, since the Fifth Classic was the work of Confucius himself.

In these classics, so Confucius taught, reside infallible guides for the life of the superior man.

The first of the *Five King* is the *Yi King*, or The Book of Changes, which is considered of great antiquity, dating back, perhaps, to the beginning of Chinese civilization, some thirty-three centuries B.C. Greater of interest than its antiquity is the fact that The Book of Changes is not a book in our sense of the word. It is a collection of eight triagrams and sixty-four hexagrams, consisting of straight lines, broken and unbroken, to which were assigned meanings fixed with mathematical precision. Each of the triagrams and hexagrams was, in fact, similar to certain symbols in higher mathematics, but infinitely more complex. The claim has often been made by the Chinese that The Book of Changes contains all human knowledge, including the modern abstract sciences—if one could only read it. But, alas, the exact meaning of the triagrams and hexagrams has been forgotten. And for centuries they were used in magic and divination. In the eleventh century B.C., two celebrated kings wrote mystical explanations of The Book of Changes, and later other scholars added their interpretations. These Confucius studied, and added some explanations of his own. He was convinced of the omniscience preserved in this classic, and that the problem was only one of time enough to study it. "If I had fifty years to study the *Yi*," he wrote, "I might come to be free from serious error."

Here is an example of one of the hexagrams, the *Li Hexagram* found in The Book of Changes, gathered and preserved by Confucius:

———————
———————
———————
——— ———
———————
———————

The meaning of this hexagram, according to the theory of symbols, if put into words, would fill a small volume. (1) The first line, (by its position and because it is unbroken) signifies that the subject is treading his accustomed path; if he should go forward, there will be no error. (2) The second line (by its position and because it is unbroken) signifies that the subject, treading a path that is level and even, is a quiet and solitary man, who, if he remains firm and holds to propriety, will gain good fortune. (3) The third line (from the bottom up, by its position and because it is broken) signifies a one-eyed man who thinks he can see; a lame man who thinks he can walk; one who treads on the tail of a tiger and is bitten.

It indicates ill fortune. (4) The fourth line (by its position and because it is unbroken) shows its subject treading on the tail of the tiger. Though he is full of apprehensive caution, he will come in the end to good fortune. (5) The fifth line (by its position and because it is unbroken) signifies that its subject treads resolutely. And though he is firm and determined, there will be peril for him. (6) And the sixth line (by its position and because it is unbroken) signifies that we must look at the entire course followed and examine the forebodings. If it is complete and without failure, it will lead to good fortune.

This, and a great deal more, one can read in the Li Hexagram, and in the other triagrams and hexagrams—if only one knows how to read them. Innumerable claims have been made about these mystic diagrams, including the claim that Confucius invented some of them himself. They are today revered as sacred symbols, and Chinese scholars pore over them to probe their meaning.

The second book of the *Five King* is the *Shu King*, or The Book of Annals, which is a fragmentary history of China, devoted principally to the record of several dynasties and their kings. The book is divided into five parts, covering the dynasties of Yao, Yu, Hsia, Shang and Chau; but the most complete and most consistent record is that of King Yao, who ruled about twenty-four centuries B.C. Confucius, who so venerated tradition, considered the knowledge of the history of the ancients a prerequisite for the "superior man."

The third book of the *Five King* is the *Shih King*, or The Book of Odes. Confucius was convinced that if a man read poetry daily, he would do no wrong. The best of poetry was in the classics. And tradition ascribes to him the task of selecting from several thousand ancient poems the 300 he included in The Book of Odes. "If you do not learn the *Shih*," he told his pupils, "you will not be fit to converse with." The collection in The Book of Odes contains ritual songs, festival songs, hymns and eulogies. But many are so profoundly human and universal in theme and treatment that they are startlingly appealing. They dwell on separation, on longing, on love. In these poems Confucius found topics, as he put it, "well fitted to rouse the mind, assist observation, make people be social, arouse virtuous indignation."

The fourth book of the *Five K'ing* is called the *Li K'ing*, or The Book of Ceremonies. And this has been called the Confucian Leviticus. That Confucius, who disclaimed any attempt to teach religion, should have included The Book of Ceremonies along with The Book of Odes was apparently meant to underscore his devotion to ritual and ceremony. For central in the education of the "superior man" was propriety based upon tradition. To do the right thing was, of course, the primary principle; but the right thing had to be done in the right way. And the right way, in Confucianism, is the traditional and ritualistic way. The ceremony of an act was not an embellishment, it was an essential part of it. The danger, and Confucius realized it, was that people would accept the form and the ritual, while neglecting the essence and the spirit; and against this he often warned his disciples.

The fifth book of the classics is the *Ch'un Ch'iu*, or Spring and Autumn, written by Confucius himself, which is really an attempt to bring the historic record in The Book of Annals up to his own times. This is the least of the *Five K'ing*.

To the *Five K'ing*, which in Confucianism assume canonical status, four apocryphal works have been added, known as the Books of the Philosophers. And among these we find the *Lun Yu*, or The Analects of Confucius, a book held in especial esteem by Confucians. And with good reason; for here we find the sayings of the Great Philosopher brilliantly and clearly stated. Collectively they present a firm and consistent ethic by which men may live in peace and dignity; in which men pledge their allegiance to principles, not persons; and once the "superior man" understands what is right, it becomes his duty to do it. "To see what is right and not to do it, that is cowardice," Confucius taught.

The following sayings, taken from The Analects of Confucius, are arranged in sequence, as they appear in the book of twenty chapters, and the chapter from which they are taken is given at the end of each saying. There is a constant reference in these sayings to the "superior" and "inferior" man or the "noble" and "small-minded" man, which frequently corresponds to the "wise" and "foolish" man in, for instance, the *Dhammapada;* more often, not wisdom or foolishness are meant but the quality of character, as in the saying, "When the inferior man does a wrong thing, he is sure to gloss over it." The terms "superior man" and "inferior man" are therefore retained throughout, and the reader can judge where it implies wisdom and where it implies nobility of character.

Although there are a number of English translations of the Analects, they are startlingly diverse. In this book the translation as given in *Sacred Books of the East,* edited by Max Muller and translated by William Jennings, was followed, and changes made only where clarity of thought seemed to require it.

Sayings from the ANALECTS

1. To learn and then to practice what one has learned, does not this bring with it a sense of satisfaction? (I)

2. Men of superior mind busy themselves first getting at the root of things; when they succeed, the right course is open to them. (I)

3. Seldom are fine words and a studied mien associated with the right feeling. (I)

4. I daily examine myself on three points: In planning for others, have I failed to be conscientious? In my dealing with friends, have I failed to be sincere? In teaching, have I failed to practice what I have taught? (I)

5. If the great man is not grave, he will not be respected; neither can his learning be solid. (I)

6. Give a prominent place to loyalty and sincerity. (I)

7. When you have erred, be not afraid to correct yourself. (I)

8. If for three years a son follows in his father's footsteps, he may be called a dutiful son. (I)

9. One excellent way to practice the Rules of Propriety is to be natural. (I)

10. When truth and right go hand in hand, a statement will bear repetition. (I)

11. The superior man, when eating, craves not to eat to the full. (I)

12. Poor yet happy; rich yet courteous. (I)

13. Sorrow not because men do not know you; but sorrow that you know not men. (I)

14. To govern simply by statute and to maintain order by means of penalties, is to render the people evasive and devoid of a sense of shame. (II)

15. If you observe what people take into their hands, observe the motives, note what gives them satisfaction; then will they be able to conceal from you what they are? (II)

16. Be versed in the ancient lore, and familiarize yourself with the modern; then you may become teachers. (II)

17. The superior man is not one-sided. (II)

18. Study without thought is a snare; thought without study is a danger. (II)

19. When you know a thing, maintain you know it; when you do not, acknowledge it. This is the characteristic of knowledge. (II)

20. Of the many things you hear, hold aloof from those that are doubtful, and speak guardedly with reference to the rest; then your errors will be few. (II)

21. Let the leader of men promote those who have ability, and instruct those who have it not, and they will be willing to be led. (II)

22. I know not what men are good for on whose word no reliance can be placed. How can the carriage be made to go without a yoke or whipple-tree? (II)

23. To see what is right and not to do it, that is cowardice. (II)

24. The superior man is not contentious. He contends only as in competitions of archery; and when he wins he will present his cup to his competitor. (III)

25. A man without charity in his heart, what has he to do with ceremonies? A man without charity in his heart, what has he to do with music? (III)

26. If you do not partake in an offering, it is as if you did not offer it. (III)

27. He who has sinned against Heaven has none other to whom his prayer may be addressed. (III)

28. Hitting the mark is what counts in archery and not piercing the target. (III)

29. It is social good feeling that gives charm to a neighborhood. (IV)

30. I have not yet seen a lover of philanthropy who did not take occasion to magnify that virtue in himself; nor a hater of misanthropy who did not, at times, indulge in something savoring of misanthropy. (IV)

31. Tell me, is there anyone who is able for one whole day to apply the energy of his mind to virtue? It may be that there are such, but I have never met with one. (IV)

32. If we may learn what is right in the morning, we should be content to die in the evening. (IV)

33. The scholar who is intent upon learning the truth, yet is ashamed of his poor clothes and food, is not worthy to be discoursed with. (IV)

34. The superior man thinks of his character; the inferior man thinks of his position; the former thinks of the penalties for error, and the latter, of favors. (IV)

35. The constant chase for gain is rich with ill-will. (IV)

36. One should not be greatly concerned at not being in office, but rather about the requirements in one's self for that office. Nor should one be greatly concerned at being unknown, but rather with being worthy to be known. (IV)

37. The superior man seeks what is right; the inferior one, what is profitable. (IV)

38. When you meet with a man of worth seek to attain his level; when you meet with a man of worthless character, examine your own heart. (IV)

39. In ancient times people were reluctant to speak, fearing that their deeds would not be as good as their words. (IV)

40. The superior man is slow to promise, prompt to fulfill. (IV)

41. Virtue dwells not in solitude; she must have neighbors. (IV)

42. Officiousness, in service, leads to disgrace; among friends, to estrangement. (IV)

43. To stand up before men and pour out a stream of glib words is one way to make yourself obnoxious to them. (V)

44. Rotten wood cannot be carved. (V)

45. In my first dealings with a man, I listen to his avowals

and trust his conduct; after that I listen to his avowals and watch his conduct. (V)

46. I have never seen a man of inflexible firmness. (V)

47. These are the four essential qualities of the superior man; he is humble, he is deferential to superiors, he is generously kind, and he is always just. (V)

48. Those who are willing to forget old grievances will gradually do away with resentment. (V)

49. I have not yet seen the man who can see his errors so as inwardly to accuse himself. (V)

50. The superior man helps those whose need is urgent, and not the rich to be richer. (VI)

51. Who can forever walk out by the door of virtue? (VI)

52. Where plain naturalness is more in evidence than fine manners, we have the country man; where fine manners are more in evidence than plain naturalness, we have the townsman; where the two are equally blended we have the ideal man. (VI)

53. Better than the one who knows what is right is he who loves what is right. (VI)

54. To prize the effort above the prize, that is virtue. (VI)

55. The superior man might be induced to go, but not to go down; he may be misled, but not fooled. (VI)

56. How far-reaching is the moral excellence that flows from the Constant Mean! (VI)

57. I am a transmitter and not an originator; I am one who believes in and loves the ancients. (VII)

58. What you find in me is a quiet brooder and memo-rizer, a student never satiated with learning, an unwea-ried monitor to others. (VII)

59. These things weigh heavily upon my mind: failure to improve in the virtues, failure in discussion of what is learned, inability to walk always according to the knowl-edge of what is right and just, inability to reform what has been amiss. (VII)

60. Fix your mind on truth; hold firm to virtue; rely upon loving-kindness; and find your recreation in the Arts. (VII)

61. Broach no subject to those who are not eager to learn. (VII)

62. If wealth were an object that I could go in quest of, I should do so even if I had to take a whip and do groom's work. (VII)

63. With coarse food to eat, water to drink, and a bent arm for a pillow, happiness may still be found. (VII)

64. If I had fifty years to study the *Yi K'ing* (The Book of Changes), I might come to be free from serious error. (VII)

65. Strange occurrences, exploits of physical strength, deeds of lawlessness, and references to mystical things—these Confucius avoided in discussion. (VII)

66. Let there be three men walking together, and in them I will be sure to find my instructors. For what is good in them I will follow; and what is not good I will try to modify. (VII)

67. Heaven produced the good that is in us. (VII)

68. The teacher should keep four things constantly in mind: his scholarship, his conduct, his integrity, and his loyalty. (VII)

69. Sift out the good from the many things you hear, and follow them; sift out the good from the many things you see and remember them. (VII)

70. If I err, however secretly, others are sure to know it. (VII)

71. Lavish living renders man disorderly; miserliness makes them hard. Better the hard than the disorderly. (VII)

72. The superior man is always calm, the inferior (small-minded) man is constantly in a state of disturbance. (VII)

73. Without a sense of proportion, courtesy becomes oppressive; calmness becomes bashfulness; valor becomes disorderliness; and candor becomes rudeness. (VIII)

74. People may be put on the way they are to follow; but they cannot be put on the way to understanding. (VIII)

75. The man who has studied for three years and found nothing for his toil would be hard to find. (VIII)

76. Even if a person were adorned with the gift of the Duke of Chau, if he is proud and avaricious, all his other qualities are not really worth looking at. (VIII)

77. If you do not occupy the office, devise not its policy. (VIII)

78. Learn as if you could never overtake your subject, yet as if apprehensive of losing it. (VIII)

79. Confucius barred four words from his speech: "Shall," "must," "certainly," and "I." (IX)

80. Confucius was free of four things: prejudice, foregone conclusions, obstinacy, and egotism. (IX)

81. At the time when I was not called upon to use my proficiencies, I acquired them. (IX)

82. Blade, but no bloom, or bloom with no fruit, that is the way of some men. (IX)

83. Topics on which Confucius rarely spoke were: Advantage, Destiny and Duty of man to man. (IX)

84. When you have erred, be not afraid to correct yourself. (IX)

85. It is easier to carry off the chief commander of an army than to rob one poor fellow of his will. (IX)

86. The wise escape doubt; the good escape trouble; the bold escape fear. (IX)

87. Some may study side by side and yet be far apart when they come to the logic of things. (IX)

88. We are so inept in serving the living, how shall we then serve the spirits? (XI)

89. We know so little about life, how can we then know about death? (XI)

90. To go beyond the mark is as bad as to fall short of it. (XI)

91. If a man can subdue his selfishness for one full day everyone will call him good. (XII)

92. Use not your eyes, your tongue, nor a limb of your body without propriety. (XII)

93. When you leave your house, go out as if to meet an important guest. (XII)

94. Do not set before others what you yourself do not like. (XII)

95. Where there is difficulty in doing, will there not also be difficulty in explaining? (XII)

96. The man with whom slander and calumny gains no currency may be called enlightened. (XII)

97. The essentials of good government are: a sufficiency of food, a sufficiency of arms, and the confidence of the people. If forced to give up one of these, give up arms; and if forced to give up two, give up food. Death has been the portion of all men from of old; but without the people's trust nothing can endure. (XII)

98. A tiger's or a leopard's skin might be a dog's or a sheep's, when stripped of its hair. (XII)

99. Whom you love you wish to live; whom you hate you wish to die. (XII)

100. The superior man makes the most of other people's good qualities, not the worst of their bad ones. (XII)

101. Hold fast to what is good and the people will be good. The virtue of the good man is as the wind: and that of the bad man, as the grass. When the wind blows, the grass must bend. (XII)

102. Is not putting duty first and success second a way of raising the standard of virtue? (XII)

103. Knowledge of man, that is wisdom. (XII)

104. In the society of books the superior man selects many

of his friends; in the society of friends, he promotes good-will among men. (XII)

105. Excuse small faults. (XIII)

106. The superior man feels reserved in matters which he does not understand. (XIII)

107. If terms are used incorrectly, language becomes incongruous. (XIII)

108. If the ruler of men is a lover of righteousness, his people will be submissive. (XIII)

109. Let the leader show rectitude in his personal character, and things will go well even without directions from him. (XIII)

110. Let good men manage a country for a century, and crime will disappear from that land. (XIII)

111. Do not wish for speedy results nor trivial advantages: speedy results will not be far-reaching; trivial advantages will matter only in trivial affairs. (XIII)

112. The Duke of Sheh once said to Confucius, "There are some honest persons in my province. If a father has stolen a sheep, the son will give evidence against him." Confucius commented, "The honest in my province are different. The father will hold a thing secret on his son's behalf; and the son does the same for his father. They are both on their way to become honest."

113. Whoever is virtuous intermittently will live to be ashamed of it. (XIII)

114. The superior man will be agreeable even when he disagrees; the inferior man will be disagreeable even when he agrees. (XIII)

115. Confucius was asked, "Is a good man one who is liked by everybody?" He answered, "No." "Is it one who is disliked by everybody?" He answered, "No. He is liked by all the good people and disliked by the bad." (XIII)

116. The superior man is easy to serve, but hard to please. The inferior man is hard to serve, but easy to please. (XIII)

117. The superior man can be dignified without being proud; the inferior man can be proud without being dignified. (XIII)

118. To lead an untrained army to war, that is wasteful slaughter. (XIII)

119. In a country of good government, the people speak out boldly and act boldly. (XIV)

120. Good men speak good words, but not all who speak good words are good. Good men are courageous, but not all courageous men are good. (XIV)

121. Can one refuse to work for those he loves? (XIV)

122. It is as hard to be poor without complaining as to be rich without becoming arrogant. (XIV)

123. That man may be regarded as perfect who seeing advantage for himself, is mindful of what is righteous; being in danger, risks his life; bound by an agreement, never forgets its conditions. (XIV)

124. He who promises without modesty will fulfill them with difficulty. (XIV)

125. The superior men are sparing in their words and profuse in their deeds. (XIV)

126. These mark the superior man: he is sympathetic

without anxiety, wise without skepticism, brave without fear. (XIV)

127. My great concern is not with men who do not know me, but with men who cannot understand me. (XIV)

128. Confucius was asked, "What say you of the remark, 'Repay enmity with kindness'?" And he replied, "How then would you repay kindness? Repay kindness with kindness, and enmity with justice." (XIV)

129. Be truthful and honest in all you say and do and, even if your country is inhabited by barbarians, you will make your way. (XV)

130. Not to teach a man who can be taught, is to waste a man; to teach a man who cannot be taught, is to waste words. The wise will lose neither men nor words. (XV)

131. There have been men who have wrecked their own lives in the endeavor to reach perfection. (XV)

132. A workman who wants to do his work well must first prepare his tools. (XV)

133. Those who care not for the morrow will soon have their sorrow. (XV)

134. I have not yet met the man who loves virtue as he loves beauty. (XV)

135. The superior man is exacting with himself; the inferior man is exacting with others. (XV)

136. The superior man does not promote a man because of his words; nor is he heedless of his words because of the man. (XV)

137. Confucius was asked, "Is there one word that sums up the basis of all good conduct?" And he replied, "Is not

'reciprocity' that word? What you yourself do not desire, do not put before others." (XV)

138. Impatience with little things makes confusion in great plans. (XV)

139. Not to retract after committing an error is in itself an error. (XV)

140. The superior man deliberates how he may walk in truth, not upon what he may eat. (XV)

141. The superior man may not be conversant with petty details, yet can be entrusted with important matters; the inferior man may be conversant with petty details yet cannot be entrusted with important matters. (XV)

142. Where instruction is to be given, there must be no distinction of persons. (XV)

143. Where men's methods are not identical, there can be no planning by one on behalf of the other. (XV)

144. In speaking, lucidity is all that is needed. (XV)

145. When the empire is well-ordered, the common people do not discuss public matters. (XVI)

146. There are three kinds of pleasure which are profitable, and three that are detrimental. The pleasure of music and ceremony, the pleasure of speaking of the goodness of others, and the pleasure of wise friends, are all good. The pleasure of wild sensuousness, of idleness, and of indulgent feasting, are detrimental. (XVI)

147. Three things the superior man guards against: lusts of the flesh in youth, combativeness in maturity, and ambition in old age. (XVI)

148. The superior man must be mindful of nine things: to be clear in vision, quick to listen, genial in expression, respectful in manner, true in utterance, serious in duty, inquiring in doubt, self-controlled in anger, just and fair when the way to success is open before him. (XVI)

149. Only the supremely wise and the abysmally ignorant do not change. (XVII)

150. To kill a cock, why use an ox-knife? (XVII)

151. If you show dignity, you will not be mocked; if you are indulgent, you will be heard; if you are faithful, you will be trusted; if you are kind, men will gladly serve you. (XVII)

152. What is white may be stained without being made black. (XVII)

153. Listening on the road, and whispering it in the land, this is abandonment of virtue. (XVII)

154. Does Heaven ever speak? The four seasons come and go, and all creatures thrive and grow. Does Heaven ever speak! (XVII)

155. It is better to play dice than to do nothing at all. (XVII)

156. A superior man dislikes many things: He dislikes to talk of other men's misdeeds; he dislikes to hear defamatory gossip by inferiors of their superiors; he dislikes those who are not brave yet have no regard for propriety; and he dislikes hasty decisions by people of limited intellect. (XVII)

157. Servants are difficult to handle. Approach them with familiarity and they will take liberties; keep them at a distance and they will grumble. (XVII)

158. If you take no liberties, your liberties will not be curtailed. (XVIII)

159. The student who daily realizes how much he has yet to learn, but forgets not what he has already learnt, is a lover of learning. (XIX)

160. Wide research and steadfast purpose, eager questioning and close reflection, all these tend to harmonize a man. (XIX)

161. Mourning should cease when the grief is past. (XIX)

162. What harm can a man do to the sun or the moon by wishing to stop either in its course? It only shows that he knows not his own limitations. (XIX)

163. In the use of words one should forever be guarded. Because of one word a man might be judged wise; and because of one word a man might be judged foolish. (XIX)

164. Confucius was asked, "What say you are the essentials of good government?" He answered, "The ruler should esteem the five excellences and avoid the four evils. The five excellences are: plentitude without extravagance; taxation without exciting discontent; desire without covetousness; dignity without haughtiness; majesty without fierceness. The four evils to be avoided are: without instruction in the law, to inflict punishment—that is tyranny; without proper warning to expect perfect adherence—that is oppression; late in giving orders and expecting early obedience—that is robbery; to tax and to spend in a stingy manner—that is a misuse of government function." (XIX)

165. He who does not recognize the existence of a Divine Law cannot be a superior man. (XIX)

The Sayings of

HINDUISM

True religion is to love, as God loves
them, all things, whether great or
small. (*Hitopadesa*)

HINDUISM

Hinduism is the Western term used to describe the very old and very complex religion accepted by the majority of the people of India. In its earlier stages it was known as Brahminism, which, in the course of many centuries, has gone through great reformations. Two of its reformers, Gautama the Buddha and Vardhamana Mahavira, eventually established two new religions, Buddism and Jainism, based on Brahminism. But most of the reformers remained within the fold and gradually transformed Brahminism from a variety of nature worship into a great macrocosmic philosophy, with monotheistic implications.

We can trace the growth and development of Hinduism in its sacred books. The earliest Sanskrit texts of Hinduism are The Books of Holy Knowledge or *Vedas*. The number of these sacred books is very large, and the best-known among them is the *Rig-Veda*, which consists of over a thousand hymns, addressed to many nature gods— the most devotional addressed to Indra, the God of the Sky, and Agni, the God of Fire. Of singular interest is Hymn 129 in the tenth section of the *Rig-Veda*, because it presents the story of creation as revealed, according to the Hindus, about 12,000 years ago. (This hymn is given in full on page 118, as translated by Ralph T. Griffith, President of Benares College, India, about a century ago.)

The next stage in the development of Hinduism is represented by the *Brahmanas*, which are commentaries on the *Vedas;* and in them nature worship is gradually transformed into a complex and theistic vision of the universe. The third stage is revealed in the *Upanishads,* which means, "A sitting down under a master," which were transmitted at first orally by priests, who considered them too sacred to be repeated in the presence of lower castes. Later the *Upanishads* were written down in books but were still reserved for an inner circle of the upper castes. The *Upanishads* are mystic speculations of a lofty nature, and they form the basis of modern Hindu philosophy.

Though Hinduism has gone through many changes since the creation of the *Rig-Vedas,* some of its basic beliefs have remained constant throughout the centuries; and even the reformers of Hinduism who founded new religions, retained these basic tenets as axiomatic principles. They are: *The Eternal Nature of the World*—the belief that the world always was and always will be; *Reincarnation*—the belief that when people die their souls are reborn into another body; *Karma*—the Law of the Deed, which establishes that when people are good in one life, they are compensated for it in their next incarnation, and when they are evil, they are punished in their next incarnation; *Nirvana*—the state of souls which have been continuously good in successive incarnations and no longer need be reincarnated—a state of perfection in nonbeing. Hinduism also retains the belief in the caste system, although this is rejected by most of its reformers. The division of people into castes, so Hinduism teaches, was determined by Brahma the Creator, and no one can change a man's caste but himself. By being continually good, the individual assures being incarnated into a higher caste.

Every follower of Hinduism strives to reach *Nirvana.* What he ought to believe and do to achieve this ultimate end is elaborately detailed in the *Brahmanas* and *Upani-*

shads and their voluminous commentaries. But nowhere are the teachings of Hinduism better summarized than in the apocryphal *Bhagavad-Gita,* or Song of the Lord, and in the wisdom-lessons of the *Hitopadesa,* or the Book of Good Counsel.

The
CREATION HYMN

(From the *Rig-Veda*)

Then was not non-existent nor existent: there was no realm of air, no sky beyond it.

What covered in, and where and what gave shelter? Was water there, unfathomed depth of water?

Death was not then, nor was there aught immortal: no sign was there, the day's and night's divider.

That One Thing, breathless, breathed by its own nature: apart from it was nothing whatsoever.

Darkness there was: at first concealed in darkness this All was indiscriminated chaos.

All that existed then was void and formless: by the great power of Warmth was born that Unit.

Thereafter rose Desire in the beginning-Desire, the primal seed and germ of Spirit.

Sages who searched with their heart's thought discovered the existent's kinship in the non-existent.

Transversely was their severing line extended: what was above it then, and what below it?

There were begetters, there were mighty forces, free action here and energy up yonder.

Who verily knows and who can here declare it, whence it was born and whence comes this creation?

The Gods are later than this world's production. Who knows then whence it first came into being?

He, the first origin of this creation, whether he formed it all or did not form it,

Whose eye controls this world in highest heaven, he verily knows it, or perhaps he knows not.

The
BHAGAVAD-GITA

There are two apocryphal epics in Hindu literature that have had as profound an influence on the followers of Hinduism as any of their sacred books. The first, and the lesser in length and influence, is called *Ramayana,* or The Adventures of Rama, and relates, in almost twenty-four thousand stanzas, the adventures of the God Vishnu, the Preserver, when in his Seventh Incarnation he appeared as Prince Rama to save the world from evil. The second and longer epic (which contains over 110,000 couplets) is called *Mahabharata,* or The Great History of the Brothers, and relates the events of another Incarnation of the God Vishnu, this time as Krishna, who was brought up as a cowherd and who participated in many important events and exploits before he was accidentally shot by a hunter and returned to the Sea of Milk, his heavenly abode.

In the *Mahabharata,* as in the *Ramayana,* is embedded a great if fanciful part of the early history of India. But that is not why the epic is so highly regarded. In the *Mahabharata* there is a record of an eighteen-day battle, and during this battle one of the generals, Arjuna, discusses the meaning of life and death with his charioteer, Krishna. Their discussion is known as *Bhagavad-Gita,* or simply *Gita.* And it is because of the *Gita* that the entire epic has assumed its unique place in Hinduism. The very reading of this epic, or any part of it, is now considered an act of faith. The epic itself records that, "The reading of the *Mahabharata* destroys all sin and creates virtue"— "The saying of a single stanza is enough to wipe away much evil."

The *Gita,* about as long as the Book of Job in the Bible, is the part of the epic which has held its high place in India from generation to generation. Mahatma Ghandi wrote in *Young India,* "When disappointment stares me in the face and all alone I see not one ray of light I go back to the Bhagavadgita. I find a verse here and verse there and I immediately begin to smile in the midst of overwhelming tragedies—and my life has been full of external tragedies—and if they left no visible, no indelible scar on me, I owe it all to the teachings of the Bhagavadgita." Like Ghandi, many of his countrymen in the past and in the present found and find solace in the *Gita.*

Selections from the *Gita* are given here, freely rendered and arranged in sequence as they appear, and they are based on Sir Edwin Arnold's translation of the *Bhagavad-Gita.*

The Sayings of

HINDUISM

1. The wise in heart mourn not for those who live, nor those who die.

2. To man's frame as there come infancy and youth and age, so come raisings-up and layings-down of other life-abodes.

3. The soul which is not moved, that takes sorrow and takes joy indifferently, lives in the life undying.

4. Birthless and deathless and changeless remains the spirit, dead though the house of it seems.

5. As one lays away a worn-out robe and takes a new one, so the spirit puts by its garment of flesh and passes to inherit a new one.

6. Weapons cannot reach the Life, nor flame burn it, nor waters overwhelm it, nor dry winds wither it. Impenetrable, unassailed, untouched, immortal, invisible, ineffable, by word and thought uncompassed, ever all itself is the soul.

7. If you hear that the man newly dead is like the man newly born, will you weep? The end of birth is death; the end of death is birth: this is ordained.

8. The birth of living things comes unperceived; the death comes unperceived; between them, beings perceive.

9. If, knowing your duty and task, you bid duty and task go by—that is sin.

10. Infamy is worse for men of noble blood than death.

11. Those who wealth and power do most desire have least hold on heavenly meditation.

12. Find the reward of doing right, in right. Let right deeds be your motive, not the fruit that comes from them.

13. Makes your acts your piety.

14. The right act is far less than the right-thinking mind.

15. Scorn those who follow virtue for her gifts.

16. With perfect meditation comes the perfect act.

17. Because they seek no gain, the right-hearted rise more certainly from the bands of body, step by step, to the highest bliss.

18. In sorrows not dejected, in joys not overjoyed; outside the stress of passion, fear and anger; steadfastly calm in lofty contemplation; such a one is the wise man.

19. He is wise who draws away his five frail senses from the world which assails them, as the tortoise draws its feet beneath the safety of its shell.

20. The governed mind may sometimes feel the sense-storms sweep, and self-control wrested by the roots. Let him regain his kingdom!

21. That man alone is wise who remains master of himself.

22. Pondering on objects of the senses gives rise to attraction; from attraction grows desire, desire flames to passion, passion breeds recklessness; and then betrayed memory lets noble purpose go, and saps the mind, till purpose, mind and man are all undone.

23. Lo! Tranquillity comes to him who deals with objects of the senses not loving and not hating, making them serve his free soul, which remains serenely lord.

24. The mind that follows the senses sees its helm of wisdom torn away, and, like a ship in a storm, drives to wreck and death.

25. Only he who is not swayed by things of the senses shows perfect wisdom.

26. What seems as wakeful day to the thick night of ignorance, is known for night to the true-seeing eyes of the wise man, just as what seems midnight-gloom to unenlightened souls shines like wakeful day to his clear gaze.

27. He who shakes off the yoke of flesh lives as lord, not servant, of his lusts.

Selections from Chapter III:
Virtue in Work

28. No man shall escape from acting by shunning action; and none shall come by mere renunciation to perfection.

29. Thought is act in fancy.

30. He who, with strong body serving mind, gives up his mortal powers to worthy work, not seeking gain, such a one is honorable.

31. Do your allotted task! Work excells idleness.

32. Do your earthly duty free from desire, and you shall well perform your heavenly purpose.

33. He who does not help to turn the rolling wheels of this great world, lives a lost life, shameful and vain.

34. In performance of plain duty man mounts to his highest bliss.

35. By works alone the ancient saints reached blessedness!

36. Even as the unknowing toil, wedded to the senses, so let the enlightened toil, sense-freed.

37. Let each play his part in all he finds to do, with unyoked soul.

38. It is better for one to do his own task as he may, even though he fail, than take tasks not his own, though they seem good.

39. To die performing duty is no ill.

40. As the womb envelops the unborn child, so is everything in this world enclosed in the desire of the flesh.

41. Resist the false, soft sinfulness which saps knowledge and judgment.

42. The world is strong, but what discerns it stronger, and the mind strongest; and high over all the ruling soul.

SELECTIONS FROM CHAPTER IV:
RELIGION OF KNOWLEDGE

43. When Righteousness declines, when wickedness is strong, I rise, from age to age, and take visible shape,

and move a man among men, succoring the good, thrusting the evil back and setting Virtue on her seat again.

44. Many there are who come, from fear set free, freed from anger and desire; keeping their hearts fixed upon me —my faithful—purified by knowledge.

45. To learn which work saves one must rightly meditate on these three: Doing, not doing and undoing.

46. He who sees how action may be rest and rest action —he is wisest among his kind; he has the truth. He does well acting or resting.

47. That man is called wise who is freed in all his works from the prickings of desire, and is burned clean in act by the fire of truth.

48. The one whose soul is free, whose heart is set on truth—of such a one what work he does is work of sacrifice, which passes purely into ash upon the altar.

49. Some votaries serve the gods with flesh and altar-smoke, but others light subtler fires and make a purer rite with will of worship.

50. The one who makes no sacrifice, he has no part or lot even in this world.

51. The sacrifice which knowledge pays is better than the great gifts offered by wealth.

52. Knowing truth, your heart will ache no more with error.

53. If you were the worst of all wrong-doers, the ship of truth would bear you safe across the sea of your transgressions.

54. The flame of knowledge burns away the dross.

55. There is no peace, no hope, nor happiness for him who doubts.

56. Cut with the sword of wisdom the doubt that binds your heart! Cleave the bond born of ignorance!

SELECTIONS FROM CHAPTER V:
RENUNCIATION OF REWARD

57. To cease from works is well, and to do works in holiness is well; but of these two the better way is his who works piously.

58. He who is fixed in holiness, self-ruled, pure-hearted, lord of sense and of self, lost in the common life of all who live—he is a saint.

59. The votaries who renounce the fruit of deeds gain endless peace.

60. Mankind errs by folly, darkening knowledge.

61. The world is overcome even here by those who fix their faith on unity.

62. Be not overglad attaining joy, and be not oversad encountering grief.

63. The joys which spring from the senses breed sure griefs.

64. Blessed is the man who learns, even while he lives and bears his body's chain, to master lust and anger.

SELECTIONS FROM CHAPTER VI:
RELIGION BY SELF-RESTRAINT

65. The perfect Yogin acts unmoved by passions and unbound by deeds, setting results aside.

66. He is the Yogi, glad with joy of light and truth, with senses subjugated, to whom the clod, the rock, the glistening gold all seem as one. By this sign is he known, being of equal grace to friends, strangers, lovers, enemies, aliens and kinsmen; loving all alike, evil or good.

67. But for earthly needs religion is not his who too much fasts or too much feasts, nor his who sleeps away an idle mind; nor his who wastes his strength in vigils.

68. Call that true piety which most removes earthly-aches and ills, where one is moderate in eating and in resting; measured in wish and act; sleeping betimes, and waking betimes for duty.

69. See! Steadfast a lamp burns sheltered from the wind; such is the likeness of the Yogi's mind, sheltered from the storms of the senses and burning bright to Heaven.

70. As often as the wild and wavering heart breaks from control, so often recurb it and rein it back to the control of the soul.

71. Perfect bliss grows only in the heart made tranquil, the spirit free from passion and purged from offense.

72. Beyond denial man's heart is hard to restrain, and wavering; yet it grows restrained by habit, by the use of self-control.

73. He who should fail, desiring righteousness, comes at death to the Region of the Just; dwells there measureless

years, and being born anew, begins life again in some fair home among the mild and happy. And so he strives anew to perfectness, with better hope.

SELECTIONS FROM CHAPTER VII:
RELIGION BY DISCERNMENT

74. Of many thousand mortals, one, perhaps, strives for truth.

75. I am the good sweet smell of the moistened earth, I am the fire's red light, the vital air moving in all that moves, the holiness of hallowed souls, the root undying, from which has sprung whatever is.

76. Hard it is to pierce that veil divine which hides me; yet those who worship me pierce it and pass beyond. I am not known to evil-doers, nor to foolish ones, nor to the base and churlish.

77. Four sorts of mortals know me: he who weeps, the man who yearns to know, he who toils to help and he who sits certain of me, enlightened.

78. Hard it is to find the wise Mahatma, the man who says, "All is Krishna."

79. There are those whose knowledge, turned aside by this desire or that, leads them to serve some lower gods, with various rites, constrained by that which molded them. To all such—worship what shrine they will, what shapes, in faith—'tis I who give them faith! I am content!

80. All creatures live bewildered, except some few who, quit of sin, holy in act, informed, steadfast in faith, cling to me.

Selections from Chapter VIII:
Religion by Devotion

81. In happy peace the faithful one does die.

82. The worlds—even Brahma's world—roll back again from death to life's unrest; but those who reach to me, taste birth no more.

83. Higher, deeper, innermost, abides another life, not like the life of the senses, escaping sight, unchanging. This endures when all created things have passed away.

Selections from Chapter IX:
Religion by the Kingly Knowledge

84. To those blessed ones who worship me, turning not otherwise, with minds set fast, I bring assurance of full bliss beyond.

85. Whoever offers me in faith and love a leaf, a flower, a fruit, or water poured forth, that offering made lovingly, with pious will, I accept.

86. Whatever you do, eating or sacrificing, giving gifts, praying or fasting, let it all be done for me.

87. I am alike to all! I know not hate, I know not favor!

88. Those who worship me with love, I love; they are in me, and I in them.

89. If an evil man turns in his thoughts to me, count him among the good; he has chosen the high way; he shall grow righteous before long; he shall attain that peace which does not change.

90. Be certain that none can perish, trusting me.

91. You who have come into this sorrowful and fleeting world set your faith fast on me.

92. Make me your supreme joy, and to my rest your spirits shall be guided.

SELECTIONS FROM CHAPTER XII:
RELIGION OF FAITH

93. Cling to me. Clasp me with heart and mind; so shall you dwell surely with me on high.

94. He who labors right for love of me shall finally attain. But, if in this your faint heart fails, bring me your failure!

95. Find refuge in me. Let the rewards of labor go, renounce hope for me, with humble heart, so shall you come; for, though to know is more than diligence, yet worship is better than knowing, and renunciation, better still.

96. Near renunciation—very near—dwells eternal peace.

97. He who hates naught of all that lives, himself compassionate, exempt from arrogance and love of self, unchanged by good or ill; patient, contented, firm in faith, master of himself, true to his word, seeking me, heart and soul; vowed to me—that man I love.

98. He who troubles not his kind, and is not troubled by them; free of wrath, living too high for gladness, grief or fear—that man I love.

99. He who dwells quiet-eyed, stainless, serene, well-balanced, unperplexed, working with me, yet from all works detached—that man I love.

100. He who, fixed in faith on me, dotes upon none, scorns none; rejoices not and grieves not, letting good or evil light when it will, and when it will, depart—that man I love.

101. He who, to friend and foe, keeping an equal heart, with equal mind bears shame and glory; with an equal peace takes heat and cold, pleasure and pain; abides freed of desires, hears praise or calumny in passionless restraint, unmoved by each; linked by no ties to earth, steadfast in me—that man I love.

102. Most of all I love those happy ones who live in single fervid faith and love unseeing, drinking the blessed ambrosia of my being.

SELECTIONS FROM CHAPTER XIII:
SEPARATION OF MATTER AND SPIRIT

103. Loving solitude, and shunning the noise of foolish crowds; resolute endeavor to reach perception of the utmost soul, and grace to understand the gain it were so to attain—that is true wisdom. And what is otherwise is ignorance.

104. Close to all, to each, yet measurelessly far! Not manifold, and yet subsisting still in all that lives; forever to be known as the Sustainer, yet, at the end of times, he makes all end—and re-creates.

105. Know that nature and the spirit both have no beginning.

106. Some few by meditation found the soul; and some by long philosophy and holy life reach there; some by works;

some, never so attaining, hear of light from other lips, and seize, and cling to it worshiping; yes, and those—to teaching true—overpass death.

107. He sees indeed who sees in all alike the living, lordly soul, supreme, imperishable amid the perishing.

SELECTIONS FROM CHAPTER XIV:
SEPARATION FROM THE QUALITIES

108. Passion, being kin to appetite, and breeding impulse and propensity, binds the embodied soul.

109. Ignorance, begot of darkness, blinding mortal men, binds down their souls to sloth and stupor.

110. Passion binds by toilsome strain; but ignorance, which shuts out the beams of wisdom, binds the soul to sloth.

111. Where darkness and dullness, sloth and stupor are, it is ignorance that has caused them.

112. The fruit of lust is pain and toil.

113. The fruit of ignorance is deeper darkness.

114. Gloom, bewilderment and ignorance grow forth from ignorance.

115. The one whose deep-seeing eyes regard the clod, the marble and the gold as one; whose heart holds the same gentleness for lovely and unlovely things, firm-set, well-pleased in praise and blame; content with honor or dishonor; tolerant alike to friend and foe; detached from undertakings—he is called Surmounter of the Qualities.

SELECTIONS FROM CHAPTER XVI:
THE HOLY AND THE PROFANE

116. Equanimity, and charity which spies no man's faults; and tenderness toward all who suffer; a contented heart, fluttered by no desires; a bearing mild, modest and grave, with manhood nobly mixed, with patience, fortitude and purity; an unrevengeful spirit, never given to rate itself too high; such are the signs of him whose feet are set on that fair path which leads to heavenly birth.

117. Those of little wit, dark-minded, give themselves to evil deeds.

118. This lie leads to death, that finds in pleasure all the good there is, and cries, "Here it finishes!"

119. Ensnared in nooses of a hundred idle hopes, slaves of passion and anger buy wealth with their base deeds to glut hot appetites.

120. The doors of hell are threefold, through which men to ruin pass—the door of lust, the door of wrath, the door of avarice.

SELECTIONS FROM CHAPTER XVII:
THE THREEFOLD KINDS OF FAITH

121. The faith of each believer conforms itself to what he truly is.

122. Purity, rectitude and no injury to any helpless thing —these mark the true religious act.

123. Words that cause no woe, words always true, gentle

and pleasing words, and those murmured in the reading of a Sacred Writ—these mark the true religious speech.

124. Serenity, benignity, sway of the silent spirit, constant stress to sanctify the nature—these mark the true religious mind.

125. Religion shown in act of proud display is rash and vain.

126. The gift lovingly given, when he who takes can render nothing back; made in due place, due time and to a meet recipient, is a gift fair and profitable.

127. The gift selfishly given, or when some end is sought, or where the gift is proffered with a grudge, is stained with impulse, ill.

128. The gift churlishly flung, at evil time, in wrongful place, to base recipient, made in disdain or harsh unkindliness, is a gift dark; it does not bless.

SELECTIONS FROM CHAPTER XVIII:
DELIVERANCE AND RENUNCIATION

129. Abstaining from a work by right prescribed never is meet.

130. Abstaining from attachment in the work, while yet one does it faithfully, saying, "It is right to do," that is true act and abstinence.

131. Being in the body, none may stand wholly aloof from acts; yet, he who abstains from profit of his acts is abstinent.

132. The fruit of labors, in the lives to come, is threefold

for all men—desirable, and undesirable, and mixed of both; but no fruit is at all where no work was.

133. True knowledge is to see one changeless life in all the lives, and in the Separate, One Inseparable.

134. Imperfect knowledge sees the separate existences apart, and, being separated, holds them real.

135. There is false knowledge: that which blindly clings to one as if it were all, seeking no Cause, deprived of light, narrow and dull, and "dark."

136. Right action is wrought without attachment, passionlessly, for duty, not for love, nor hate, nor gain.

137. Good is the intellect which comprehends the coming forth and going back of life, what must be done, and what must not be done, what should be feared, and what should not be feared, what binds and what emancipates the soul.

138. Good is the steadfastness by which a man masters his heartbeats, his very breath of life, the action of his senses; fixed in never-shaken faith.

139. Stained is the steadfastness by which a man holds to his duty, purpose, effort, end, for life's sake, and the love of goods to gain.

140. Sad is the steadfastness with which the fool clings to his sloth, his sorrow, and his fears.

141. Good pleasure is the pleasure that endures, banishing pain forever; bitter at first as poison to the soul, but afterward sweet as the taste of ambrosia. Drink of that!

142. Painful pleasure springs from the bond between the senses and the sense-world. Sweet as ambrosia is its first taste, but its last is bitter as poison.

143. A Brahman's virtues, born of his nature, are serenity, self-mastery, religion, purity, patience, uprightness, learning, and to know the truth of things which be.

144. A Kshatriya's pride, born of his nature, lives in valor, fire, constancy, skilfulness, spirit in fight, and open-handedness and noble mien, as of a lord of men.

145. A Vaisya's task, born with his nature, is to till the ground, tend cattle, venture trade.

146. A Sudra's state, suiting his nature, is to minister.

147. He who performs, diligent, content, the work alotted him, whatever it may be, lays hold of perfectness.

148. Better your own work, though done faultily, than doing others' work, even excellently.

149. In your thoughts do all you do for me.

150. In faith of me all dangers you shall vanquish, by my grace; but, trusting to yourself, and heeding not, you can but perish.

151. There lives a Master in the hearts of men who makes their deeds, by subtle pulling-strings, dance to what tune he will.

152. Cling in faith and love and reverence to me. So shall you come to me.

153. Fly to me alone! Make me your single refuge! I will free your soul from all its sins.

The HITOPADESA

If the *Bhagavad-Gita* presents a profound search for universal truths, the *Hitopadesa* seeks, in a light vein, the wisdom by which man can be governed in his daily activities.

The *Hitopadesa*, or The Book of Good Counsel, is written in the tradition (or is a later version) of the *Panchatantra*, considered the source of all animal fables. Originally, as explained in the opening of the *Hitopadesa*, the book was designed for the training of certain princes, the sons of King Sundarsana, in the wisest way of ruling with justice. The wise teacher, Visnu-Sarman by name, instructed the princes by telling them a long sequence of amusing fables, and each fable concluded with a wisdom-lesson, formulated in a couplet.

The fables of the *Hitopadesa* are known and loved throughout India, and their wise conclusions are quoted on many occasions, especially when instructing the young. While the fables in the *Hitopadesa* are woven into a chain, so that the end of one serves as the beginning of the next, and their conclusions alone are no substitute for the entertaining and delightful fables, yet, as wisdom literature, they can be read and appreciated in themselves. Here are given one-hundred-and-one wisdom-lessons taken from the *Hitopadesa*.

The Sayings from the
HITOPADESA

1a. Wise men live each day as if Death's fingers were already entwined in their hair.

2a. Better than the best of riches is wisdom—for once won, none may lose her again.

3a. Wisdom is like a seeing eye—he who has her is not blind.

4a. Are you childless? Less the misery of the childless than the misery of the father of a fool.

5a. One wise son makes his father glad; forty fools avail him nothing.

6a. The five joys of life are his who has: ease, health, reverent children, wisdom, and a soft-voiced wife.

7a. If you treat Fortune like a master, she will serve you like a slave.

8a. Fate and Will run together.

9a. Destiny is master today—Man was master yesterday.

10a. Worthy ends do not come about from wishing.

11a. In the company of the wise even fools may attain to wisdom.

12a. The wise are free of a thousand sorrows and a hundred dreads that each day trouble foolish heads.

13a. Good things do not issue out of bad things.

14a. Nectar mixed with poison still serves no purpose but to kill.

15a. Medicine is good for the sick, but good for nothing for those who are healthy.

16a. Even when his Scripture learning is astonishing, the cheat remains a cheat.

17a. Be wary of rivers, weapons, horned creatures, women, and the sons of kings.

18a. Avarice breeds anger and blind desires, and is the fruitful mother of a countless spawn of sin.

19a. Be second and not first: the share is the same if all goes well; and if not, the first is to blame.

20a. When the shadow of the cloud of danger hovers it dims the mind.

21a. Passion is the slave or the mistress: followed she will bring but sorrow; lead her, and you tread the path of fortune. Choose the way that you will go.

22a. The noble soul is not elated in good fortune, in misfortune not dismayed; always eloquent in council; fearless always in the fight; proud of honor; steadfastly on wisdom set.

23a. As furious elephants can be secured with ropes of grass-blades, so small things grow mighty when cunningly combined.

24a. If you strip off the rice-husk, the rice-grain will not grow.

25a. Sickness, anguish, bonds and sorrow spring from wrongs done long ago.

26a. Death, that must come to all, comes nobly if we give our possessions and our life to help men live.

27a. Are you my faithful friend? Then guard my honor!

28a. Kind greetings, a place to rest in, fire, and water—these simple gifts are freely given wherever good men dwell.

29a. Whoever your guest may be, rich man or beggar, honor him for your own honor's sake.

30a. Do not withhold your compassion from those who ask for it: does not the holy moon shine equally on the leper and on the lord?

31a. When the poor are roughly turned away from your gate, they carry off your good deeds with them, and upon you lay their sins.

32a. In the house the husband rules; men call the Brahman 'master'; but the guest is lord of them all.

33a. Enemy is friend, and friend is enemy—as our actions make them so.

34a. Where there are no wise men, men of little wit are lords.

35a. He is the true friend who is beside us when trouble comes our way.

36a. The love of a faithful wife remains constant whatever the husband loses or wins.

37a. The one who shares his comrade's portion, and comes

as surely to the battle as to the festive board—he is friend and kinsman.

38a. The tongues of flatterers are like daggers in our absence, but in our presence, softer than silk.

39a. Shun flatterers when they promise little, and shun them when they promise much, for, enkindled, charcoal burns, and cold, charcoal defiles the touch.

40a. Where there are no wise men, men of little wit are lords.

41a. The deed proves the promise.

42a. Noble hearts are like golden vessels—for close is the bond of true metals.

43a. Evil hearts are like earthen vessels—they crack and break at a touch.

44a. One foot goes, and one foot stands, when the wise man leaves his lands.

45a. The hero's stalwart arm and steadfast spirit win a home for him wherever he goes.

46a. Feeble folk are poor folk.

47a. When money goes, wit goes with it.

48a. Wealth is title to respect and fame and wisdom—that it should be so is shame.

49a. Empty is the childless home.

50a. Poverty can slay a hundred virtues.

51a. Knowledge half known, pleasure purchased with future sorrow, and the salt of servitude—these are the greatest griefs.

52a. When you have the golden gift of contentment, you have everything.

53a. When the soul, serene, can spurn hope's elusive dreams, all is known, digested, tested; nothing new is left to learn.

54a. Have you never waited for the great man's door to be unbarred? Or never lingered saying a last sad parting word? Spoke you never one light thing you would recall? Rare your life has been and fair your fortune!

55a. True religion is to love, as God has loved them, all things, whether great or small.

56a. What is bliss? When a sane mind fills a healthy body.

57a. To know what is good and what is ill, that is true knowledge.

58a. Two fair blossoms grow upon the tree of life: one, the company of good men; and the other, the sweet songs of poets.

59a. Give, and your wealth shall grow; give, and you shall the more safely keep the wealth you have.

60a. The miser who hides his treasure in the earth opens up a passage for his soul to sink to hell.

61a. The man who keeps his coins for counting and not for barter or for alms, though he may breathe like a blacksmith's bellows, that man in truth is not alive.

62a. Gifts which are bestowed with kindness make the giving doubly dear.

63a. Studied wisdom when unapplied avails nothing.

64a. Fortune enters the happy dwelling of those careless of her favor, and who stand unafraid.

65a. Though wealthy, be not haughty; though you have lost all, do not despair; for fate plays with our mortal fortunes as a child plays with a ball.

66a. Worldly friendships, women, youth, new corn, and riches—these are quickly passing pleasures.

67a. Be not over thoughtful for your bread—God has taken thought for all: when the babe is born to the mother's breast sweet milk is brought.

68a. He who gave her silver to the swan, her plumes of pride to the hawk, and his purples to the peacock—He will verily provide.

69a. Even for good ends, on wealth do not waste a minute; though mud may be wiped off, wise men do not plunge within it.

70a. Oh, the gleaming arrows of a fair woman's eye! Feathered with her lovely lashes, how perilously they pass us by.

71a. Homely features do not lack favor when they reveal true wisdom.

72a. A wife is beautiful and honored when her heart is staunch and true.

73a. What force would never try may be achieved by fraud.

74a. 'Friend'! The heart can hardly tell whence came this jewel of a word to men.

75a. Men of little store are great when looking down on

lives below them; but hard to each man seems his fate when looking up to higher fortunes.

76a. In the path to greatness are these obstructions sent: sloth, illness, sleeping, servitude to woman, and complacency.

77a. Observe how the ant-hill grows, adding little to little—live, give, learn, as life goes.

78a. Little gains accumulate to make large stores.

79a. Though men may spin their cunning schemes—God knows who shall lose or win.

80a. Many prayers are uttered for the one on whom many lives depend.

81a. By their own deeds men go downward, and by their own deeds upward they mount.

82a. As down hill rushes the rock which uphill was hard to roll, so the soul quickly sinks to vice, which to virtue slowly rises.

83a. He who speaks unasked, or comes unbid, or counts on favor—will be rebuked.

84a. Pitiful is the one who fearing failure, makes no beginning.

85a. Nearest to the king is dearest.

86a. Women, vines, and princes, twine round that which grows nearby.

87a. A fool may step on jewels and lift glass to his crown; yet jewels always remain jewels, and glass for jewels never pass.

88a. Neither disparagement nor slander can kill the spirit of the brave.

89a. Strength serves reason.

90a. He who thinks a minute little, like a fool an hour misuses.

91a. To your heart this lesson take—fools suffer for their folly.

92a. The fire never tires of burning, or death of slaying, or the sea of drinking rivers, or lovely woman of betraying.

93a. Flee from the house that has false friends, impudent servants, and a brawling wife.

94a. Strength is his who has sense; the fool is weak.

95a. Long-tried friends are the friends to cling to.

96a. An evil soul raised to honor still retains his evil bent.

97a. Even though watered with nectar, the poison-tree bears deadly fruit.

98a. Guard the seed of counsel within the husk of silence.

99a. Before you scorn your enemy find out who are his friends.

100a. Pain and pleasure are allied.

101a. May friendship never be parted, save among the evil-hearted.

The Sayings of

JAINISM

"All living beings hate pain;
therefore one should not injure them
or kill them. This is the essence
of wisdom: not to kill anything."
Sutra-krit-anga

JAINISM

The wisdom of one of the living religions is summed up in a single word. The name of that religion is Jainism, and the word is *Ahimsa*. Literally translated the word means "non-injury"; but its meaning implies "reverence for life." Jainism as a religion and as an ethical system is, of course, a mansion with many chambers, but its cornerstone is *Ahimsa*.

Jainism, like Buddhism, arose as a reform movement of Brahminism, and its early history so closely resembles the early development of Buddhism that when Western scholars examined the two, they were inclined at first to look upon them as either two branches of the same movement or as outgrowths one from the other. But a closer examination of their teachings soon revealed basic differences.

During the lifetime of Prince Gautama (who became the Buddha) in the northern kingdom of the Sakyas, another prince lived in the neighboring kingdom of Mogadah, whose name was Vardhamana, and whom the people called Mahavira, the Great Hero. This name was given him quite early by his people, when in his youth he exhibited exemplary courage, compassion and modesty.

Prince Gautama renounced his luxurious life in the palace when he was twenty-nine years old and, as a beggar-monk, sought enlightenment; Mahavira was twenty-eight when, stricken with grief at the death of his parents, he began to brood about the meaning of life and death, then joined an order of beggar-monks and took a vow of silence for twelve years. For twelve years he meditated, and at the end of that time he had clarified to himself many fundamental assumptions as found in Brahminism, and from them he reached a number of new conclusions of his own. When his vow of silence was fulfilled he went out to teach the people his doctrine. And for thirty years he taught among the people, who now called him the Lord Mahavira. His disciples gathered his teachings, sermons and discourses into forty-six books, written in Prakrit, a northern or common form of Sanskrit. These books, called the *Agamas*, became the sacred scriptures of Jainism.

The fundamental assumptions of Jainism are: that Matter is atomic in structure and is eternal; that Time is eternal and passes in cycles of inconceivably long duration, one cycle slowly rising to a peak of goodness, then declining and entering into another cycle, which progressively descends into evil until it reaches the lowest depths of depravity before turning up again toward a new cycle of goodness. These successive cycles are measured in quintillions of centuries.

How man, whose life is less than a wink in an aeon of time, can live so as to find peace for his soul and escape the suffering of the world, is the concern of the complex teachings of Jainism. From the parent religion Jainism accepts as axiomatic that all living things are *reincarnated;* that *Karma,* the Law of the Deed, operates in all lives, and that for whatever good or evil one does in one life, one will be rewarded or inexorably punished in the next life; and that the ultimate aim of all beings is to reach the state of nonbeing, in the eternal peace of *Nirvana. Nirvana* could be reached, Lord Mahavira taught, by the acceptance of the Three Jewels of the Soul: *Right Conviction, Right Knowledge* and *Right Conduct.* The last, Right Conduct, comes first, because salvation cannot be achieved through prayer, through sacrifices, through the worship of many

gods or through holy men, but only through good deeds
done with understanding and conviction. "Within yourself lies salvation," he taught; and each man can attain salvation through his good deeds.

But where the Buddha taught that the good deed is
always far from extremes and defined The Middle Path
as the road for men to follow, Lord Mahavira accepted
the extreme of asceticism and self-denial, defined in his Five
Commandments, of which the first and most important is
Ahimsa—noninjury to anything that has life, because
everything that lives has a soul.

Naturally the following of Lord Mahavira remained
small, since his followers, having accepted *Ahimsa,* could
not go to war, they could not hunt or fish, they could not
exterminate pests, they could not eat meat in any form,
they could not cook food after sunset, for moths might be
attracted to the fire and perish; they could not even walk
about at night or after a rain lest they might inadvertently
step on worms. There are about one-and-a-half million
followers of Jainism in India today. Because of the tenets
of their religion they are unable to engage in farming,
since in tilling the soil insects would be killed; they are
unable to become butchers, fishermen, brewers, gunmak-
ers or enter any other occupation which might ultimately
lead to the destruction or injury of any living creature.
Most Jainists in India are merchants and bankers. But any
financial success they may achieve is not spent on luxurious living. They give much of their wealth for splendid
temples and a great variety of homes for the sick or the
aged. They even have homes for sick and aging animals
and insects. Daily they engage in the duty of giving
charity. And all their actions follow logically from their
complete reverence for all things living, their motivations
deeply rooted in the implicit belief of *Ahimsa.*

Foremost among the Jainist sacred books are the
Twelve Angas, of which the second, the *Sutra-krit-anga,*

has the primary task of fortifying young monks in their faith, but along the way it covers a multitude of subjects which reveal and summarize the essential teachings of Jainism. The *Sutra-krit-anga* is divided into two books, each of which contains an unequal number of lectures, which, in turn, are divided into chapters. The sayings from the *Sutra-krit-anga* which have been selected to represent the essential wisdom of Jainism, are based on the Hermann Jacobi translation from the Prakrit. The source of each selection is indicated by book, lecture and chapter (where lectures are given in more than one chapter), and verses.

The Sayings of

JAINISM

1. Know what causes the bondage of the soul; and knowing, try to remove it. (I:1;1;1)

2. All things are eternal by their very nature. (I:1;1;16)

3. As the swift deer without protection are often frightened where there is no danger, and not frightened where there is danger, and therefore are caught in the snare, so some who hold the wrong doctrine are often afraid of what is free from danger, and not afraid of real dangers. (I:1;2;6-10)

4. The fool dreads the preaching of the Law, but not the works, being without discernment or knowledge. (I:1;2; 11)

5. The speculation of agnostics cannot lead to knowledge. (I:1;2;17)

6. As those who are guided by a blind man, are they who seek salvation but follow the false Law. (I:1;2;19-20)

7. As imprisoned birds do not get out of their cage, so those ignorant of right or wrong do not get out of their misery. (I:1;2;22)

8. There are three ways of committing sins: by our own actions; by authorizing others; and by approval. (I:1;2; 26)

9. The mind of those who sin in thought is impure. (I:1; 2;29)

10. Those who in arguments of their own maintain that the world has been created, do not know the truth. (I:1; 3;9)

11. Misery arises from wicked deeds. (I:1;3;10)

12. A sage leads a life as far removed from love as from hate. (I:1;4;2)

13. The world is boundless and eternal; it exists for eternity and shall not perish. (I:1;4;6)

14. All living beings hate pain: therefore do not injure them or kill them. This is the essence of wisdom: not to kill anything. (I:1;4;9-10)

15. Leave off pride, anger, deceit and greed. (I:1;4;12)

16. It is difficult to obtain instruction in the Law after this life. (I:2;1;1)

17. Men suffer individually for the deeds they themselves have done. (I:2;1;4)

18. Even an ascetic will be severely punished for his deed when he engages in deceit. (I:2;1; 7)

19. The wise man should consider that not he alone suffers; all creatures in the world suffer. (I:2;1;13)

20. To blame others leads to no good. (I:2;2;2)

21. Even he who is the servant of a servant, if he observes the vow of silence, has no reason to be ashamed. (I:2;2;3)

22. The wise man who can see far into the past and the future will practice indifference. (1:2;2;4)

23. Conceit is a very thin thorn; it is difficult to pull out. (I:2;2;11)

24. The sage does not fear for his life, nor does he desire praise for his courage. (I:2;2;16)

25. A wise man never quarrels. (I:2;2;19)

26. Though life cannot be prolonged, still foolish people sin recklessly. (I:2;2;21)

27. Those who are not subdued by pleasures know meditation to be their duty. (I:2;2;27)

28. The pious should not tell stories, ask idle questions, or engage in gossip. (I:2;2;28)

29. Virtuous men regard pleasures as equal to diseases. (I:2;3;2)

30. Discipline yourself! The wicked strongly grieve, groan and wail. (I:2;3;7)

31. Though your life lasts a hundred years, you die like the short-lived man; the years swiftly pass. (I:2;3;8)

32. Knowing the truth, one should live up to it. (I:2;3;15)

33. The fool thinks that his wealth, cattle and kin will save him; they him, or he them. (I:2;3;16)

34. If you are intent on your spiritual welfare, do not kill any living beings by your acts, by your orders, or by your consent. (I:2;3;21)

35. A man considers himself a hero as long as he does not behold the foe. (I:3;1;1)

36. When the battle is begun, the mother will not recognize her son. (I:3;1;2)

37. Like fish in shallow water, the weak become disheartened by the heat of summer. (I:3;1;5)

38. Begging is a hard task. (I:3;1;6)

39. Weak men are disheartened by reproof, as cowards in battle. (I:3;1;7)

40. A cow which has just calved does not stray far. (I:3;2; 11)

41. Kings and ministers of kings try to seduce with pleasant things the man who leads a holy life. (I:3;2;15)

42. At the time of battle the coward looks behind him for a ditch. (I:3;3;1)

43. The arguments of him whose mind possesses good qualities proceed in a way that does not exasperate his opponent. (I:3;3;19)

44. The ignorant are easily led astray. (I:3;4;1)

45. If you hold fast to what is wrong you will regret it, like the man who carried iron a long way believing it was silver. (I:3;4;7)

46. Women are to the foolish a temptation, difficult to resist. (I:3;4;16)

47. They who spend much time with women cease to practice meditation. (I:4;1;16)

48. Women have one man in their heart, another in their words, and still another in their arms. (I:4;1;24)

49. The second folly of the sinner is that he obstinately denies what he has done. (I:4;1;29)

50. Some supporters of their sons carry burdens like camels. (I:4;2;16)

51. He who kills or injures for the sake of his comfort will sink to a place of torture at the end of his life. (I:5;1;4-5)

52. As thunder is the loudest of sounds, as the moon is the most glorious of heavenly bodies, and as sandalwood is the best of perfumes, so is he who has renounced all desires. (I:6;19)

53. Every being, born high or born low in the scale of living creation, will meet with death. (I:7;3)

54. He who lights a fire kills living beings; he who extinguishes it kills the fire. Therefore a wise man who considers the Law should light no fire. (I:7;6)

55. Reckless men who cut down sprouts out of regard for their own pleasure, destroy many living creatures. (I:7;8)

56. If perfection could be obtained by ablutions, many creatures living in water must have reached perfection. (I:7;14)

57. Those who have not learned the truth will come to harm. (I:7;19)

58. The servile may say flattering things for the sake of food, but wrong belief and bad conduct are as worthless as chaff. (I:7;26)

59. No man should seek fame and respect by his austerities. (I:7;27)

60. Men appear in two classes: one says exertion consists in works, and the other, in abstention from works. (I:8;2)

61. As a tortoise covers its limbs with its own shell, so the wise man should cover his sins with his own meditation. (I:8;16)

62. Do not spread your own fame. (I:8;24)

63. A pious man eats little, drinks little, sleeps little. (I:8; 25)

64. A wise man should abstain from: shoes, an umbrella, dice, chowries, working for another. (I:9;18)

65. A wise man should abstain from: fame, glory, and renown; honors, respectful treatment, and all pleasures of this world. (I:9;22)

66. A secret should never be revealed. (I:9;26)

67. People should be approached impartially: one should not do anything either to please or to harm them. (I:10;7)

68. The foolish man is full of selfishness; he toils day and night, greedy for wealth, as if he will never grow old or die. (I:10;18)

69. A man should treat all creatures in the world as he himself would like to be treated. (I:11;33)

70. A blind man, though he may carry a light, still does not see. (I:12;8)

71. Always honor the man who is like a light and makes manifest the Law. (I:12;19)

72. Those who speak falsely from pride of knowledge are not capable of many virtues. (I:13;3)

73. He who is quarrelsome is not impartial. (I:13;6)

74. He who is carried away by passion will not get very far. (I:14;7)

75. He who has lost his way should treat with honor him who has not. (I:14;11)

76. Though fearless, be modest. (I:14;22)

77. He who always knows the truth is kind to his fellow-creatures. (I:15;3)

78. He who is purified by meditation is like a ship in the water that avoids all dangers until it reaches the shore. (I:15;5)

79. There have been wise men who, having come to the end, made the end manifest. (I:15;25)

80. There are five elements through which we explain whether an action is good or bad; earth, water, fire, wind and air. Everything, down to a blade of grass, consists of these five elements. (I:1;21-22)

81. Men of good character and morals are easy to please. (II:2;75)

82. He who recognizes that he sins and does not cease from sinning is called a foolish man. (II:2;78)

83. There were three hundred and sixty-three philosophical schools, and their founders differed in intellect, will, character, taste, understanding and plans; and all formed into one circle and each one stood in his place. Then a man, carrying with a pair of iron tongs a vessel full of burning coals, asked the philosophers to take the vessel from him with their bare hands for only a moment. But the philosophers held back, because, they said, if they took it their hands would burn and cause them pain. Then said the man, "This is a maxim of general application, a true principle of religious reflection: all creatures are averse to pain. They who cause pain to any creature will in time-to-come suffer a variety of pains." (II:2;79-80)

84. Though a fool does not consider the operations of his mind, speech, and actions, still he commits sin. (II:4;5)

85. Do not maintain that the world is an illusion; maintain that it exists. (II:5;13)

86. Do not maintain that love and hate do not exist, but that they do exist. (II:5;22)

87. Do not maintain that there is no such thing as good or evil, but that there is good and evil. (II:5;28)

The Sayings of

JUDAISM

Do not unto others that which is
hateful to you. This is the whole
of the Law; all the rest is
commentary. *Rabbi Hillel, Talmud*

JUDAISM

The essence of Judaism lies in its teachings on the search for a way of life in which every human being is held equally sacred, and that the fulfillment of each life is to be attained in good deeds joyfully performed. Judaism is a religion of practice and not faith only; and the practice of Judaism, its teachings stress, can be accomplished only with great joy. "Tears may open the gates," one saying goes, "but laughter will tear down the very walls." A universalist ethic permeates Judaism, which prescribes in great detail how one ought to live in a world which is God's gift to mankind, and insists upon a moral code governing man's behavior from the cradle to the grave. Adherence to this moral code constitutes adherence to the religion. Good deeds, enjoyment of living and love of mankind are the keys to the good life. All the rest is elaboration.

But the elaboration of what constitutes a good deed in practice; the limitations of enjoyment; and the definition of the love of mankind has, over many centuries, resulted in a voluminous body of literature, consisting of the Written Law, the Oral Law, the commentaries on each and commentaries on the commentaries. Central in this entire literature is the concept of the One-ness of God and the unity of mankind. The purpose of mankind is to serve God. Man can serve God by serving mankind joyfully.

Strangely enough, this monotheistic and universal religion became, for historical reasons, limited to a particular group of people who were unified by a purely national experience, although the ethics of Judaism could have been acceptable to vast numbers if the historical experience of the Jewish people had not been interwoven with the essentials of their religion. As an indication of this, whereas Judaism, today, has a following of less than one-half of one percent of mankind, its universal appeal was instrumental in stimulating two great religions, Christianity and Islam, which are now accepted by nearly half of mankind.

Judaism, as has often been expressed, rests on three pillars: The Law (*Torah*), The Repetition of the Law (*Mishnah*) and The Study of the Law (*Gemara*).

The Law, or *Torah*, is included in the Hebrew Bible (the Old Testament), and contains basically all the moral precepts of Judaism. In the Bible we even find the injunction that not one word may be added or taken away from the Written Law (Deut. 4:2). But by the time the Hebrew Bible was assembled, completed and established, great changes had taken place in the life of the Jews, which necessitated oral interpretation of many of the laws. Then there began a period of oral study on a vast scale, with some of the teachers promulgating new laws based upon the implications in the old laws. Several centuries of this development resulted in a collection of six "orders" or volumes (topically subdivided into sixty-three "tractates" or divisions), called the *Mishnah*. But by the time the *Mishnah* was set down on paper, the teachers of the Written Law and of the Oral Law often found it necessary to clarify these works by commentaries. The Bible and the *Mishnah* were written in Hebrew, which was the language spoken by the Jews at the time these were compiled. Later the Jews spoke Aramaic and taught in Aramaic. And their commentaries and explanations of a great part of the *Mishnah,* at that later period, resulted in a work of commentary, known in Aramaic as *Gemara*, or The Study of the Law.

The *Mishnah* text, together with the *Gemara* commentaries, which run to forty formidable volumes, are jointly known as: *Talmud*. But often the *Gemara* alone is erroneously referred to as the *Talmud*. Scholars in the schools of Jerusalem, as well as academicians who dwelt in Babylonia, simultaneously carried on the work of expounding the *Mishnah*, and their efforts resulted in *two* encyclopedic works; one known as the "Babylonian Talmud" and the other as the "Palestinian Talmud."

To these were added many supplementary works. For the *Mishnah* was no sooner completed than it was found in need of supplementary clarifications. These were called simply, "The Supplements" (*Tosefta*). Before, during and after the *Talmud* was assembled, many commentaries by a diversity of scholars made their appearance, and some, like the "Great Commentary" (*Midrash Rabah*), later came to occupy a place of importance next only to the *Gemara*.

All these works, concerned with the essential teachings of Judaism, are generally divided into two parts: the strictly theological and legal sections addressed exclusively to theologians and scholars; and the other part aimed at the layman. With the learned few the scribes and teachers had no problem, but to make the Law understandable, acceptable and unforgettable to the people, they had to resort to many literary devices.

The parable was one device often resorted to by the creators of the *Talmud*. As an example, the following parable is told, to curb excessive grieving for the dead: A certain Rabbi had two sons, and they both died suddenly while their father was at the academy. The mother placed them upon a bed and covered them with a sheet. When her husband returned home from the academy at the end of the day, she said, "My husband, the other day someone left in my charge a treasure, but now he has returned to claim it. Shall I return it or not?" The Rabbi said to her, "Is there any question about returning to the owner whatever he left with you for safekeeping?" She then took his hand and led him to the bed where the two children lay, and removed the sheet from the dead. When he began to weep, she said to him, "The Lord has given and the Lord has taken away; blessed be the name of the Lord forever!"

Some teachers used the fable as a vehicle of popularization. One famed teacher, who is known as the Jewish Aesop, created several hundred fables in which the fox impresses the lessons of the Law. To illustrate a point in his teachings he would start by telling a fable about a wise fox.

The most frequently used literary device, found alike in the Bible and the *Talmud*, is the saying. And through these sayings the ethics of Judaism were impressed upon the people. There are so many sayings in the Judaic literature that even if the selection were restricted to the Bible and the *Talmud*, an exhaustive collection would become a voluminous work. A few representative sayings have been included here from the Bible and the *Talmud* which give expression to the basic ethics of Judaism.

But all these sayings, according to tradition, stem from one source: The Ten Commandments. In them resides implicitly the whole of the Divine Law, and any man of any race who lives by them and fulfills them always is, in the eyes of the Lord, equal to the High Priest.

THE
TEN COMMANDMENTS

I AM THE LORD YOUR GOD, who brought you out of the land of Egypt, out of the house of bondage. You shall have no gods besides me.

YOU SHALL NOT MAKE ANY IMAGE or any manner of likeness of anything that is in heaven above, or on earth below, or that is in the water under the earth. You shall not bow down to them, nor serve them; for I the Lord your God am a jealous God, visiting the iniquity of the fathers upon the children to the third and fourth generation of those who hate me; but showing mercy to the thousandth generation of those who love me and keep my commandments.

YOU SHALL NOT TAKE THE NAME OF THE LORD GOD IN VAIN; for the Lord will not hold him guiltless who takes his name in vain.

REMEMBER THE SABBATH DAY, to keep it holy. Six days shall you labor and do all your work; but the seventh day is a sabbath to the Lord your God: on it you shall not do any manner of work, you, nor your son, nor your daughter, nor your man-servant, nor your maid-servant, nor your cattle, nor the stranger who is within your gates. For in six days the Lord made heaven and earth, the seas and all that is in them; and on the seventh day he rested. Therefore the Lord blessed the sabbath day and made it holy.

HONOR YOUR FATHER AND YOUR MOTHER, that your days may be long upon the land which the Lord your God gives you.

YOU SHALL NOT COMMIT MURDER.

YOU SHALL NOT COMMIT ADULTERY.

YOU SHALL NOT STEAL.

YOU SHALL NOT BEAR FALSE WITNESS against your neighbor.

YOU SHALL NOT COVET your neighbor's house; you shall not covet your neighbor's wife, nor his man-servant, nor his maid-servant, nor his ox, nor his ass, nor anything that is your neighbor's.

(Ex. 20:1-17) (Deut. 5:6-21)

The Sayings of the
OLD TESTAMENT

1. God created man in his own image, in the image of God created he him. (Gen. 1:27)

2. Dust you are, and to dust shall you return. (Gen. 3:19)

3. Am I my brother's keeper? (Gen. 4:9)

4. Shall not the Judge of all the world do justly? (Gen. 18:25)

5. Vex not a stranger, nor oppress him, for you were strangers. (Ex. 22:21)

6. You shall not follow a multitude to do evil. (Ex. 23:2)

7. You shall not take vengeance or bear any grudge against your own people, but you shall love your neighbor as yourself. (Lev. 19:18)

8. Rise up before the hoary head, and honor the face of an old man. (Lev. 19:32)

9. Have one law for the sojourner and for the native. (Lev. 24:22)

10. If your brother becomes poor and cannot maintain himself, you shall maintain him. (Lev. 25:35)

11. Open wide your hand to your brother, to the needy and to the poor. (Deut. 15:11)

12. A bribe blinds the eyes of the wise, and subverts the cause of the righteous. (Deut. 16:19)

13. Every man shall be put to death for his own sin. (Deut. 24:16)

14. Let not arrogance come from your mouth. (I Sam. 2:3)

15. The bows of the mighty are broken, but the feeble gird on strength. (I Sam. 2:4)

16. The Lord makes poor and makes rich; He brings low, He also lifts up. (I Sam. 2:7)

17. Not by strength shall man prevail. (I Sam. 2:9)

18. Wickedness proceeds from the wicked. (I Sam. 24:13)

19. Godless men are like thorns that are thrust away; for they cannot be taken with the hand; but the man who touches them arms himself with iron and the shaft of a spear. (II Sam. 23:6)

20. Eat the fat, and drink the sweet, and send portions to those for whom nothing is prepared. (Neh. 8:10)

21. The Lord gave and the Lord has taken away; blessed be the name of the Lord. (Job 1:21)

22. Surely vexation kills the fool, and jealousy slays the simple. (Job. 5:2)

23. Man is born to trouble as the sparks fly upward. (Job 5:7)

24. Happy is the man whom God corrects. (Job 5:17)

25. How forcible are upright words! (Job 6:25)

26. A stupid man will get understanding when a wild ass's colt is born a man. (Job 11:12)

27. In the thought of one at ease there is contempt for misfortune. (Job 12:5)

28. Water wears away the stones. (Job 14:19)

29. Your own mouth condemns you; your own lips testify against you. (Job 15:6)

30. Be afraid of the sword, for wrath brings the punishment of the sword. (Job 19:29)

31. The triumph of the wicked is short, and the joy of the godless but for a moment. (Job 20:5)

32. God abases the proud, but he saves the lowly. (Job 22:29)

33. The price of wisdom is above pearls. (Job 28:19)

34. To depart from evil is understanding. (Job 28:28)

35. Beware lest anger entice you into scoffing. (Job 36:18)

36. Who can number the clouds by wisdom? (Job 38:37)

37. The Earth is the Lord's, and the fullness thereof. (Psalm 24:1)

38. Weeping may endure for a night, but joy comes in the morning. (Psalm 30:5)

39. Keep your tongue from evil, and your lips from guile. (Psalm 34:13)

40. The humble shall inherit the earth. (Psalm 37:11)

41. The little a righteous man has is better than the riches of the wicked. (Psalm 37:16)

42. Cast your burden upon the Lord, and he will sustain you. (Psalm 55:22)

43. The righteous shall grow like the palm tree; he shall flourish like the cedar of Lebanon. (Psalm 92:12)

44. They who sow in tears shall reap in joy. (Psalm 126:5)

45. Except the Lord build the house, they labor in vain who build it. (Psalm 127:1)

46. As arrows in the hand of a mighty man, so are the children of one's youth. (Psalm 127:4)

47. How good and pleasant it is for brothers to dwell together in unity! (Psalm 133:1)

48. The fear of the Lord is the beginning of wisdom. (Prov. 1:7)

49. The waywardness of the thoughtless shall slay them. (Prov. 1:32)

50. Be not wise in your own eyes. (Prov. 3:7)

51. Whom the Lord loves he corrects, even as a father the son in whom he delights. (Prov. 3:12)

52. Withhold not good from him to whom it is due, when it is in the power of your hand to do it. (Prov. 3:27)

53. Say not to your neighbor, "Go, and come again, and tomorrow I will give," when you have it with you. (Prov. 3:28)

54. Devise not evil against your neighbor. (Prov. 3:29)

55. Envy not the man of violence, and choose none of his ways. (Prov. 3:31)

56. The wise shall inherit honor, but fools carry away disgrace. (Prov. 3:35)

57. Enter not into the path of the wicked, and walk not in the way of evil men. (Prov. 4:14)

58. The lips of a strange woman drop honey, and her mouth is smoother than oil; but her end is bitter as wormwood, sharp as a two-edged sword. (Prov. 5:3-4)

59. Drink waters out of your own cistern, and running waters out of your own well. (Prov. 5:15)

60. His own iniquities will ensnare the wicked, and he will be held with the cords of his sin. (Prov. 5:22)

61. Go to the ant, you sluggard; consider her ways, and be wise; who having no chief, overseer, or ruler, provides her bread in the summer, and gathers her food in the harvest. (Prov. 6:6)

62. There are six things which the Lord hates, seven which are an abomination to him: haughty eyes, a lying tongue, and hands that shed innocent blood; a heart that devises wicked thoughts, feet that are swift in running to evil; a false witness that breathes out lies, and he who sows discord among brothers. (Prov. 6:16)

63. Can a man take fire in his bosom, and his clothes not be burned? Or can one walk upon hot coals, and his feet not be scorched? So he who seeks his neighbor's wife; whoever touches her shall not go unpunished. (Prov. 6:27-29)

64. A friend loves at all times, and a brother is born for adversity. (Prov. 7:17)

65. Give to a wise man, and he will be still wiser; teach a righteous man, and he will increase in learning. (Prov. 9:9)

66. The woman Folly is clamorous; she is thoughtless, and knows nothing. And to him who lacks understanding, she says, "Stolen waters are sweet, and bread eaten in secret is pleasant." But he knows not that the dead are there; that her guests are in the depths of hell. (Prov. 9:13,17-18)

67. A wise son makes a glad father. (Prov. 10:1)

68. He who gathers in summer is a wise son, but he who sleeps at harvest is a shameful one. (Prov. 10:5)

69. Hatred stirs up strife, but love covers all sins. (Prov. 10:12)

70. The rich man's wealth is his strong city; the destruction of the poor is their poverty. (Prov. 10:15)

71. In many words there is room for sin, but he who controls his lips is wise. (Prov. 10:19)

72. Like vinegar to the teeth, and smoke to the eyes, is the sluggard to those who send him. (Prov. 10:26)

73. A false scale is an abomination to the Lord, but a just weight is his delight. (Prov. 11:1)

74. When pride comes, then comes shame; but with the lowly is wisdom. (Prov. 11:2)

75. Riches are of no avail in the day of wrath, but righteousness saves from death. (Prov. 11:4)

76. For want of guidance a people will fall, but in many counselors there is safety. (Prov. 11:14)

77. Like an ornament of gold in a swine's snout is beauty in a woman without discretion. (Prov. 11:22)

78. The generous soul shall be enriched; and he who satisfies shall himself be satisfied. (Prov. 11:25)

79. He who troubles his own house shall inherit the wind. (Prov. 11:29)

80. A good woman is a crown to her husband. (Prov. 12:4)

81. A righteous man has regard for the life of his beast, but even the tender mercies of the wicked are cruel. (Prov. 12:10)

82. The way of a fool seems right in his own eyes; he who is wise listens to counsel. (Prov. 12:15)

83. A prudent man conceals his knowledge, but the fool proclaims his foolishness. (Prov. 12:23)

84. Care in the heart of a man bows him down, but a good word makes him glad. (Prov. 12:25)

85. The sluggard desires, but gains nothing, while the diligent is amply rewarded. (Prov. 13:4)

86. Hope deferred makes the heart sick, but desire fulfilled is a tree of life. (Prov. 13:12)

87. Poverty and shame come to him who refuses correction, but he who accepts reproof shall be honored. (Prov. 13:18)

88. He who walks with wise men shall be wise, but the companion of fools shall suffer harm. (Prov. 13:20)

89. He who spares the rod, hates his son; he who loves his son chastens him betimes. (Prov. 13:24)

90. The wise woman builds her house, but the foolish one tears it down with her own hands. (Prov. 14:1)

91. The heart knows its own bitterness. (Prov. 14:10)

92. The thoughtless believe every word, but the prudent man watches his every step. (Prov. 14:15)

93. He who is soon angry deals foolishly. (Prov. 14:17)

94. The poor is hated even by his neighbor, but the rich have many friends. (Prov. 14:20)

95. In all labor there is profit, but mere talk tends only to penury. (Prov. 14:23)

96. He who is slow to anger has great understanding, but he who becomes easily angered exalts folly. (Prov. 14:29)

97. A tranquil heart prolongs life, but envy is a rot in the bones. (Prov. 14:30)

98. He who oppresses the poor blasphemes his Maker, but he who has mercy on the needy honors Him. (Prov. 14:31)

99. A soft answer turns away wrath, but harsh words stir up anger. (Prov. 15:1)

100. A merry heart makes a cheerful countenance. (Prov. 15:13)

101. All the days of the poor are sorrowful, but he of a merry heart has a continual feast. (Prov. 15:15)

102. Better a little with the fear of the Lord, than great treasure, and with it trouble. (Prov. 15:16)

103. Better a dinner of herbs where love is, than a roasted ox, with hatred. (Prov. 15:17)

104. To the wise the path of life goes upward. (Prov. 15:24)

105. The Lord is far from the wicked, but he hears the prayer of the righteous. (Prov. 15:29)

106. How much better it is to get wisdom than gold; to get understanding rather than silver. (Prov. 16:16)

107. Pride goes before destruction, and a haughty spirit before a fall. (Prov. 16:18)

108. Pleasant words are like honey, sweet to the soul and health to the body. (Prov. 16:24)

109. A perverse man sows strife, and a whisperer separates friends. (Prov. 16:28)

110. He who is slow to anger is better than the mighty, and he who rules his temper than he who conquers a city. (Prov. 16:32)

111. The lot is cast, but disposing of it is from the Lord. (Prov. 16:33)

112. Better a dry morsel in peace, than a house full of feasting with strife. (Prov. 17:1)

113. The refining pot is for silver, and the furnace for gold; but the Lord tries the heart. (Prov. 17:3)

114. A rebuke cuts deeper into one who has understanding than a hundred stripes into a fool. (Prov. 17:10)

115. Let a man meet a bear robbed of her whelps, rather than a fool bent on his folly. (Prov. 17:12)

116. He who rewards evil for good, evil shall not depart from his house. (Prov. 17:13)

117. A merry heart is good medicine, but a broken spirit dries up the bones. (Prov. 17:22)

118. Even a fool, when he holds his peace is accounted wise. (Prov. 17:28)

119. The slothful is brother to the wastrel. (Prov. 18:9)

120. The rich man's wealth is his strong city, and like a high wall in his own conceit. (Prov. 18:11)

121. Before destruction the heart of man is haughty, but before honor goes humility. (Prov. 18:12)

122. The spirit of a man will endure illness; but a broken spirit who can bear? (Prov. 18:14)

123. Death and life are in the power of the tongue, and those who indulge it shall eat its fruit. (Prov. 18:21)

124. He who finds a good wife finds a great good, and obtains favor of the Lord. (Prov. 18:22)

125. The poor entreat, but the rich answer insolently. (Prov. 18:23)

126. There are friends that one has to his own hurt; but there is a friend who sticks closer than a brother. (Prov. 18:24)

127. Wealth gains many friends; poverty separates them. (Prov. 19:4)

128. Many will entreat the favor of the noble, and everyone is a friend to him who gives gifts. (Prov. 19:4)

129. House and riches are an inheritance from fathers; a prudent wife is from the Lord. (Prov. 19:14)

130. There are many devices in a man's heart, but it is

the purpose of the Lord that shall be established. (Prov. 19:21)

131. Who can say, "I have made my heart clean, I am pure from my sin?" (Prov. 20:9)

132. The hearing ear, and the seeing eye, the Lord has made them both. (Prov. 20:12)

133. There is gold, and there are rubies; but the lips of knowledge are more precious than either. (Prov. 20:15)

134. Bread of deceit is sweet to a man, but afterwards his mouth shall be filled with gravel. (Prov. 20:17)

135. He who closes his ear to the cry of the poor shall cry out himself, but shall not be heard. (Prov. 21:13)

136. He who loves pleasure will be a poor man; he who loves wine and oil will not be rich. (Prov. 21:17)

137. It is better to dwell in a desert than with a contentious and an angry woman. (Prov. 21:19)

138. The horse is prepared for the battle, but victory is of the Lord. (Prov. 21:31)

139. A good name is more desirable than great riches. (Prov. 22:1)

140. Train a child in the way he should go, and even when he is old he will not depart from it. (Prov. 22:6)

141. The borrower is servant to the lender. (Prov. 22:7)

142. The lazy man says, "There's a lion in the street; I will be killed if I go out." (Prov. 22:13)

143. The mouth of a strange woman is a deep pit: he whom the Lord abhors shall fall into it. (Prov. 22:14)

144. Remove not the ancient landmark which your fathers have set. (Prov. 22:28)

145. Toil not to become rich, for riches can make themselves wings and fly away like an eagle toward heaven. (Prov. 23:5)

146. As he thinks in his heart, so is he. (Prov. 23:7)

147. Speak not in the ears of a fool, for he will despise the wisdom of your words. (Prov. 23:9)

148. Who has woe? Who has sorrow? Who has strife? Who has wounds without cause? Who has redness of the eyes? Those who tarry long over wine. Look not upon the wine when it is red, when it gives its color to the cup. It may slide down smoothly, but in the end it bites like a serpent, and stings like an adder. (Prov. 23:29-32)

149. Through wisdom a house is built, and by understanding it is established, and by knowledge the chambers are filled with all precious and pleasant riches. (Prov. 24:3-4)

150. If you faint in the day of adversity, your strength is small indeed. (Prov. 24:10)

151. Rejoice not when your enemy falls, and let not your heart be glad when he stumbles. (Prov. 24:17)

152. Fret not because of evil men, nor be envious of the wicked; for there is no future for the evil man; and the candle of the wicked shall be put out. (Prov. 24:19-20)

153. Be not a witness against your neighbor without cause; and deceive not with your lips. (Prov. 24:28)

154. I went by the field of the slothful, and by the vineyard of the man void of understanding. And lo, it was

overgrown with thistles, and covered with nettles, and the stone wall was broken down. Then I beheld, and considered; I saw, and received instruction. "Yet a little sleep, a little slumber, a little folding of the hands to sleep"—so shall poverty come upon you like a runner, and want, like an armed man. (Prov. 24:30-31)

155. The heaven for height, and the earth for depth, and the heart of kings, is unsearchable. (Prov. 25:3)

156. A word fitly spoken is like apples of gold in baskets of silver. (Prov. 25:11)

157. As clouds and wind without rain, so is he who boasts of a gift not yet given. (Prov. 26:1)

158. Let your foot be seldom in your neighbor's house, lest he weary of you. (Prov. 25:17)

159. Confidence in an unfaithful man in time of trouble is like a broken tooth, and a foot out of joint. (Prov. 25:19)

160. As vinegar upon a wound, so is he who sings songs to a sorrowing heart. (Prov. 25:20)

161. If your enemy is hungry, give him bread to eat, and if he is thirsty, give him water to drink: for you will heap coals of fire upon his head, and the Lord will reward you. (Prov. 25:21-22)

162. As cold water to the thirsty, so is good news from a far country. (Prov. 25:25)

163. He who cannot control his temper is like a city without defences. (Prov. 25:28)

164. Answer not a fool according to his folly, lest you also be like him. (Prov. 26:4)

165. Answer a fool according to his folly, lest he be wise in his own eyes. (Prov. 26:5)

166. He who meddles in strife not concerning him, is like one who catches a dog by the ears. (Prov. 26:17)

167. Flattering lips and a wicked heart are like an earthen vessel overlaid with silver dross. (Prov. 26:23)

168. He who digs a pit shall fall into it. (Prov. 26:27)

169. A lying tongue hates those whom it has wounded; and a flattering mouth works ruin. (Prov. 26:28)

170. Boast not of tomorrow, for you know not what the day may bring. (Prov. 27:1)

171. Let another man praise you, and not your own mouth. (Prov. 27:2)

172. Wrath is cruel, and anger is overwhelming; but who can stand before jealousy? (Prov. 27:4)

173. The sated loathe even honey, but to the hungry every bitter thing is sweet. (Prov. 27:7)

174. The eyes of man are never satisfied. (Prov. 27:20)

175. The wicked flee when no man pursues, but the righteous are bold as a lion. (Prov. 28:1)

176. Those who forsake the law praise the wicked, but those who keep the law contend with them. (Prov. 28:4)

177. He who augments his substance by usury and unjust gain, shall gather it for him who has pity on the poor. (Prov. 28:8)

178. When the righteous are in authority, the people rejoice; but when the wicked rule, the people mourn. (Prov. 29:1)

179. A man who flatters his neighbor spreads a net for his feet. (Prov. 29:5)

180. When a ruler listens to falsehood, all his servants become wicked. (Prov. 29:12)

181. Where there is no vision, the people perish. (Prov. 29:18)

182. See you a man who is hasty in his words? There is more hope for a fool than for him. (Prov. 29:20)

183. A man's pride shall bring him low, but the humble in spirit shall obtain honor. (Prov. 29:23)

184. An unjust man is abhorred by the just; and he who is upright is abhorred by the wicked. (Prov. 29:27)

185. There are three things which are too wonderful for me, yes, four which I cannot understand: the way of an eagle in the air; the way of a serpent upon a rock; the way of a ship in the midst of the sea; and the way of a man with a maiden. (Prov. 30:18-19)

186. Give strong drink to him who is ready to perish, and wine to those heavy of heart. (Prov. 31:6)

187. Open your mouth for the dumb in the cause of those appointed to destruction. (Prov. 31:8)

188. All the rivers run into the sea, yet the sea is not full; to the place from where the rivers come, there they return again. (Ecc. 1:7)

189. Is there anything of which it may be said, "See, this is new"? (Ecc. 1:10)

190. Wisdom excels folly, as light excels darkness. (Ecc. 2:13)

191. There is nothing better for a man, than that he should eat and drink, and make his soul enjoy good in his labor. (Ecc. 2:24)

192. To everything there is a season, and a time to every purpose under the heaven: a time to be born, and a time to die; a time to plant, and a time to pluck up that which is planted. (Ecc. 3:1-2)

193. A threefold cord is not quickly broken. (Ecc. 3:12)

194. Woe to him who is alone when he falls, for he has no one to help him up. (Ecc. 4:10)

195. The profit of the earth is for all: the king himself is served by the field. (Ecc. 5:9)

196. He who loves silver shall not be satisfied with silver, nor he who loves abundance, with increase. (Ecc. 5:11)

197. The sleep of a laboring man is sweet. (Ecc. 5:12)

198. A good name is better than precious ointment. (Ecc. 7:1)

199. It is better to hear the rebuke of the wise, than to hear the song of fools. (Ecc. 7:5)

200. More bitter than death the woman whose heart is snares and nets, and her hands like bands. (Ecc. 7:26)

201. God made man upright, but they have sought out many inventions. (Ecc. 7:29)

202. Whatever your hand finds to do, do with all your might. (Ecc. 8:9)

203. A living dog is better than a dead lion. (Ecc. 9:4)

204. Wisdom is better than strength. (Ecc. 9:16)

205. By slothfulness the roof caves in, and through idleness of the hands the house leaks. (Ecc. 10:18)

206. Cast your bread upon the waters: for you shall find it after many days. (Ecc. 11:1)

207. He who observes the wind shall not sow; and he who regards the clouds shall not reap. (Ecc. 11:4)

208. In the morning sow your seed, and do not rest until evening: for you know not which shall prosper, whether this or that, or whether both shall be alike good. (Ecc. 11:6)

209. Remember then your Creator in the days of your youth; before the silver cord is loosed, or the golden bowl is broken, or the pitcher is broken at the fountain, or the wheel broken at the cistern; and the dust returns to the earth as it was, and the spirit returns to God who gave it. (Ecc. 12:1;6-7)

210. Love is strong as death. (S. of S. 8:6)

211. Jealousy is cruel as the grave. (S. of S. 8:6)

212. Many waters cannot quench love, neither can the floods drown it. (S. of S. 8:7)

213. They shall beat their swords into plowshares, and their spears into pruning hooks; nation shall not lift up sword against nation, neither shall they learn war any more. (Isaiah 2:4)

214. The grass dries up, the flower fades, only the word of the Lord endures forever. (Isaiah 40:8)

215. He gives power to the faint, and to those who have no might he gives strength. (Isaiah 40:29)

216. Shall the clay say to him who fashions it, "What are you making?" (Isaiah 45:9)

217. There is no peace for the wicked. (Isaiah 48:22)

218. How beautiful upon the mountains are the feet of him who brings good tidings, who publishes peace! (Isaiah 52:7)

219. If a man falls, does he not attempt to rise again? (Jer. 8:4)

220. The stork in the heavens knows her appointed time. (Jer. 8:7)

221. Can the Ethiopian change his skin, or the leopard his spots? (Jer. 13:23)

222. What has the chaff to do with the wheat? (Jer. 23:28)

223. The fathers have eaten sour grapes, and the children's teeth are set on edge. (Jer. 31:29)

224. Every man shall die for his own sin. (Jer. 31:30)

225. As is the mother, so is the daughter. (Ezekiel 16:14)

226. They have sown the wind and they shall reap the whirlwind. (Hosea 8:7)

227. Sow in righteousness, reap in mercy. (Hosea 10:12)

228. Rend your hearts and not your garments. (Joel 2:13)

229. Will two walk together unless they are agreed? (Amos 3:3)

230. Will a bird fall in a snare upon the ground, where there is no lure for it? (Amos 3:5)

231. The lion has roared, who does not fear? The Lord God has spoken, who can but prophesy? (Amos 3:8)

232. Let justice flow like waters, and righteousness like a mighty stream. (Amos 5:24)

233. As you have done, it shall be done to you. (Obad. 1:15)

234. O man, what is good, and what does the Lord require of you? Only to do justly; to love mercy; and to walk humbly with your God. (Micah 6:8)

235. Woe to him who increases that which is not his! (Hab. 2:6)

236. Woe to him who builds a town with bloodshed! (Hab. 2:12)

237. Let none of you imagine evil in your hearts against his neighbor. (Zach. 8:17)

238. Have we not all one Father? Has not one God created us all? (Malachi 2:10)

THE SAYINGS
OF THE FATHERS

In the *Mishnah,* embedded in the legalistic volume
on "Torts," between the tract on "Idolatry" and the tract
of "Decisions" concerning inadvertent sin through the
misdirection of religious authority, we come upon a brief
collection of maxims, called The Sayings of the Fathers
(*Pirke Aboth*). This small sheaf of sayings so endeared
itself to the early leaders of Judaism that they incorpo-
rated it in its entirety into their Prayer Book. And as a
result, it is claimed, the sayings became part of both Jewish speech and life, and even the humblest worker, who
had no opportunity to study the Bible and the Talmud,
became versed in Jewish precepts through the sayings and
found in them guidance in his daily life.

The Sayings of the Fathers has become the subject
of voluminous commentaries, explaining and amplifying
the maxims and interpreting their place in Judaic ethics.
Yet they need little commentary to be understood. The
book consists of only six chapters, with eleven verses in
the shortest chapter and twenty-seven in the longest. And
it begins with the recapitulation, "Moses received the
Torah on Sinai and handed it down to Joshua; Joshua to
the elders; the elders to the prophets, and the prophets
handed it down to the Men of the Great Assembly." Then
the sayings begin, each prefixed by a preamble as to who
formulated the particular maxim, whose son he was,
whose pupil and in what city he was teaching.

The following sayings are arranged in sequence, with
identifications as to chapter and verse.

Maxims from
THE SAYINGS
OF THE FATHERS

1a. Be deliberate in judgment; gain many disciples; and build a fence around the Law. (1:1)

2a. The world rests on three things: on the Law, on service, and on charity. (1:2)

3a. Let your house be a meeting place for the wise. (1:4)

4a. He who multiplies gossip brings evil upon himself. (1:5)

5a. Provide yourself with a teacher; acquire a companion; and judge every man as if you were in his place. (1:6)

6a. Do not befriend the wicked; move away from a bad neighbor; and never lose faith in justice. (1:7)

7a. Be searching in the examination of witnesses, and be careful of your words, lest through them they learn to falsify. (1:9)

8a. Be a lover of work and a hater of lordship; and do not cater to the ruling powers. (1:10)

9a. A name made great is a name destroyed. (1:13)

10a. He who does not increase his knowledge decreases it. (1:13)

11a. Promise little and do much; and receive every man cheerfully. (1:15)

12a. In many words there is room for transgression. (1:17)

13a. Not inquiry but action is the chief thing. (1:17)

14a. The world is preserved by three things: truth, justice and peace. (1:18)

15a. All theory and no practice leads to futility. (2:2)

16a. Do not separate yourself from the community; do not trust yourself to your dying day; and judge no man until you have put yourself in his place. (2:5)

17a. In a place where there are no men, strive to be a man. (2:6)

18a. Not every man who succeeds in business is necessarily wise. (2:6)

19a. The shy cannot learn; the irracible cannot teach. (2:6)

20a. He who multiplies flesh, multiplies worms; he who multiplies property, multiplies worries; he who multiplies servants, multiplies lewdness; and he who multiplies charity, multiplies peace. (2:8)

21a. The more knowledge, the more life. (2:8)

22a. The more charity, the more peace. (2:8)

23a. Let the honor of your friend be as dear to you as your own: and do not allow yourself to be easily moved by anger. (2:15)

24a. Envy, passion and hatred drive a man toward death. (2:16)

25a. Respect your friend's property as if it were your own. (2:17)

26a. Do nothing which appears wicked in your own eyes. (2:18)

27a. The day is short, the work is great, the workers are sluggish, and the reward is high; and the Master is urgent. (2:19)

28a. It is not your duty to complete the work; but neither are you free to shirk it. (2:21)

29a. Reflect on three things, and you will not come under the power of sin: where you come from, where you are going, and before whom you will have to give an accounting. (3:1)

30a. Pray for the welfare of the government, for without it men would destroy each other. (3:2)

31a. If three have eaten at a table and have not spoken words of Law, it is as if they had eaten of sacrifices to dead idols. (3:4)

32a. He who keeps awake at night, and goes on his way alone, and turns his heart to idle thoughts, sins against himself. (3:5)

33a. God stands in the congregation of the godly. (3:7)

34a. He whose good deeds are greater than his wisdom, his wisdom will endure; he whose wisdom is greater than his good deeds, his wisdom will not endure. (3:12)

35a. Morning sleep, midday wine, childish talk, and attendance at the assemblies of the ignorant drive a man toward death. (3:14)

36a. He who profanes things sacred has no share in the world to come. (3:15)

37a. Be swift to please your elders and be affable to youth; and receive all men with joy. (3:16)

38a. From jesting to levity to lewdness. (3:17)

39a. Silence is the fence of wisdom. (3:17)

40a. Beloved is man, for he was created in the image of God. (3:18)

41a. Everything is foreseen by God, yet freedom of choice is given to man. (3:19)

42a. Where there is no Law, there are no manners. (3:21)

43a. Where there is no food, there is no study. (3:21)

44a. Without knowledge there can be no understanding; without understanding there can be no knowledge. (3:21)

45a. He whose wisdom exceeds his good deeds is like a tree whose branches are many but whose roots are few. (3:22)

46a. Who is wise? He who learns from all men. (4:1)

47a. Who is mighty? He who controls his passions. (4:1)

48a. Who is rich? He who is satisfied with his lot. (4:1)

49a. Who is honored? He who respects his fellow-men. (4:1)

50a. One good deed leads to another; one evil deed to another. (4:2)

51a. Make not the Law a crown with which to glorify yourself, nor a spade with which to dig. (4:7)

52a. He who honors the Law will himself be honored. (4:8)

53a. Judge not alone, for none may judge alone save One. (4:10)

54a. Be humble before all men. (4:12)

55a. For each good deed you gain for yourself one defender; for each evil deed you gain for yourself one prosecutor. (4:13)

56a. Be cautious when you teach; for an error in teaching may amount to the presumption of sin. (4:16)

57a. There are three crowns: the crown of wisdom; the crown of priesthood; and the crown of royalty. But the crown of a good name excels them all. (4:17)

58a. It is not in our power to explain either the prosperity of the wicked or the afflictions of the righteous. (4:19)

59a. Rather be the tail of a lion than the head of a fox. (4:20)

60a. One hour of good deeds in this world is better than the whole of life in the World to Come. (4:22)

61a. Do not try to appease your friend in the hour of his anger; to comfort him in the hour when his dead lie before him; to question him in the hour when he makes his vow; and to see him in the hour of his disgrace. (4:23)

62a. Rejoice not when your enemy falls; and let not your heart be glad when he stumbles. (4:24)

63a. If one learns as a child, to what is he likened? Like writing with ink on clean paper. If one learns as an old man, to what is he likened? To writing with ink on blotted paper. (4:25)

64a. He who learns from the young is like one who eats unripe grapes and drinks wine from the vat. (4:26)

65a. Judge not the contents by the flask: a new flask may be full of old wine; and an old flask may not have even new wine in it. (4:27)

66a. Envy, cupidity and ambition lead a man to death. (4:28)

67a. Seven traits mark the wise man and seven, the foolish: The wise man does not speak before his superior in wisdom; he does not interrupt his friend's speech; he is not hasty to answer; he questions to the point and answers to the point; he speaks on first things first and on the last, last; regarding that which he does not understand he says, 'I do not understand it'; and he always acknowledges the truth. The foolish have the opposite traits. (5:10)

68a. The sword came into the world because of delay and perversion of justice. (5:11)

69a. There are four characters among men: He who says, "What is mine is mine and what is yours is yours—his is a neutral character. (Some say this is the character of the men of Sodom.) He who says, "What is mine is yours, and what is yours is mine"—he is a boor. He who says, "What is mine is yours and what is yours is yours"—he is a saint. And he who says, "What is mine is mine and what is yours is mine"—he is a wicked man. (5:13)

70a. There are four kinds of tempers: He whom it is easy to provoke and easy to pacify—his loss disappears in his gain; he whom it is hard to provoke and hard to pacify

—his gain disappears in his loss; he whom it is hard to provoke and easy to pacify—he is a saint; he whom it is easy to provoke and hard to pacify—he is a wicked man. (5:14)

71a. There are four kinds of disciples: He who quickly understands and quickly forgets—his gain disappears in his loss; he who understands with difficulty and forgets with difficulty—his loss disappears in his gain; he who understands quickly and forgets with difficulty—he is a good disciple; and he who understands with difficulty and forgets quickly—he is a poor disciple. (5:15)

72a. There are four types of students: the sponge, the funnel, the strainer and the sieve. The sponge, which soaks up everything; the funnel which takes in at one end and lets out at the other; the strainer which permits the wine to pass out and retains the lees; and the sieve which separates the bran from the fine flour. (5:18)

73a. Be strong as a leopard, light as an eagle, fleet as a hart, and strong as a lion to do the will of your Father who is in heaven. (5:23)

74a. According to the labor is the reward. (5:26)

75a. The Law is above the priesthood and greater than royalty. (6:6)

THE TALMUD

The Talmud is the work of some two thousand teachers, over a period of five centuries, most of whom used the saying as a means of underscoring a moral principle. Collectively, their sayings cover all the fundamentals of Judaism, and emphasize, by their repetition in different forms, the concepts they considered of primary importance. Over and over again we find these concepts in the sayings: Man was given the free will to choose between good and evil; human life is sacred, and all human beings are created in God's image; faith and knowledge are virtues only if they result in good deeds; and all that comes within the definition of "charity" is the deed without equal for goodness. "Charity," a saying puts symbolically, "saves from death."

Most of the sayings in the Talmud are presented in a form that would fix them in the memory of the people by their brevity, by their brilliance and by their sound. Often a saying is reduced to three words that have an alliterative sound. Such an example is the saying to induce people to remember the three circumstances under which a man's character can best be observed: how he behaves in his cups or when drunk, how he behaves when his purse is affected and how he behaves when angered. All this was expressed, in Hebrew, in three three-syllable words having the same consonants but different vowels: *"Bekisoh, bekosoh, bekaasoh,"* meaning: "By his cup, by his purse, by his anger." This was easy to remember. More frequently the comparison was used—"Like vinegar to the teeth and smoke to the eyes is the sluggard to those who depend on him." And just as frequently they repeated a saying, giving it first in a positive form and then, with variations, in a negative form, or vice versa—"A false scale is an abomination to the Lord, but a just scale is his delight." These, and a number of other literary forms, were employed in the sayings to make them quickly grasped and long retained.

A representative sampling has been included here from the great number of sayings in the Talmud. And the source of each is given on pages 289-290.

The Sayings of the TALMUD

1b. Proclaim your virtues in a whisper, and your faults in a loud voice.

2b. Rather be the cursed than the curser.

3b. Support the poor of the Gentiles with the poor of Israel; visit the sick of the Gentiles with the sick of Israel; and give honorable burial to the dead of the Gentiles as to the dead of Israel, because that is the way of peace.

4b. Be soft as a reed, not hard like a cedar.

5b. If you pray on behalf of another, while you yourself are in need of the same thing, your need will be answered.

6b. When you pray turn your eyes downward and your heart upward.

7b. There is no sadness in the presence of God.

8b. He who makes his voice heard during prayer is small in faith.

9b. All is in the hands of Heaven, except the fear of Heaven.

10b. He who prays in a loud voice is of the prophets of falsehood.

11b. Falsehood is common, truth is rare.

12b. The punishment of the liar is that he is not believed.

13b. A judge should always imagine that a sword is pointed at his heart.

14b. No man shall die for the crime of another.

15b. A judge is forbidden to listen to one party before the arrival of the other.

16b. More important is a day of rain than the Resurrection of the Dead, since the Resurrection is for the righteous and not the wicked, whereas rain is for both the righteous and the wicked.

17b. Whoever takes a fee to adjudicate, his verdict is invalid.

18b. Why are the fingers tapered like pegs? So that they can be inserted in the ears when one hears foolishness.

19b. Silence is good for the wise; how much more so for the foolish.

20b. Neither the proud nor the angry have the power of prophecy.

21b. Silence heals all ailments.

22b. Happy is he who can ignore an insult; a hundred evils pass him by.

23b. Whoever runs after greatness, greatness flees from him; and whoever flees from greatness, greatness runs after him.

24b. Whoever practices charity and justice is as though he filled the whole world with lovingkindness.

25b. Even he who is maintained by charity must himself practice charity.

26b. True charity is practiced in secret. The best type of charity is where the person who gives does not know who receives it; and the person who receives it does not know who gave it.

27b. The salt of money is in its diminution.

28b. Cleanliness leads to purity, purity to self-control, self-control to holiness, holiness to humility, humility to fear of sin, fear of sin to saintliness.

29b. There is no suffering without iniquity.

30b. Temptation is at first like a spider's web, but in the end it is like cart-ropes.

31b. Temptation is at first like a passerby, then like a lodger, and finally like the master of the house.

32b. Temptation is at first sweet; in the end, bitter.

33b. Not the mouse is the thief, but the hole is the thief.

34b. The associate of a thief is like a thief.

35b. Slander slays three persons: the slanderer, the listener, and the slandered.

36b. Evil desires only what is forbidden.

37b. He who commits an offence and repeats it, begins to believe that it is permitted.

38b. A man is duty bound to pray for the bad, even as he prays for the good.

39b. No person commits a sin unless there enters into him a spirit of madness.

40b. Had the Torah not been given to us for our guidance, we could have learned modesty from the cat, honesty from the ant, chastity from the dove, and good manners from the cock.

41b. One self-reproach is better than many lashes.

42b. The place which the penitent occupy the righteous are unable to reach.

43b. To give oneself an air of superiority shortens a man's days.

44b. Authority buries those who assume it.

45b. He who gives vent to his anger destroys his house.

46b. The life of the irracible, the melancholy or the overly compassionate is hardly worth living.

47b. He who is good toward God and his fellowmen is the righteous man who is good; but one who is good toward God and evil toward his fellowmen is the righteous man who is not good. He who is wicked toward God and wicked toward his fellowmen is a wicked man who is evil; but he who is wicked toward God and not so toward his fellowmen is a wicked man who is not evil.

48b. Do not become intoxicated and you will not sin.

49b. God hates the man who says "yes" with his mouth and "no" in his heart.

50b. Whoever visits the sick takes away a sixtieth part of his illness.

51b. Greater is he who follows the commandments from love than he who follows them from fear.

52b. Every prophet prophesied only for the penitent.

53b. He who breaks a law to save a life is free of guilt.

54b. The world grows dark for the one who must depend upon the table of others.

55b. A man takes greater delight in one measure of his own than in nine belonging to his neighbor.

56b. Many are the friends at the palace gates; few at the gates of the debtor's prison.

57b. He who teaches the son of his neighbor is as though he were the father.

58b. A man should not say, "I will study the Scriptures that people may call me learned; I will study Mishnah that people may call me Rabbi; I will teach that I may be a Professor in the Academy."

59b. A city in which there are no schoolchildren is doomed.

60b. Study leads to practice.

61b. God weeps over three types of persons: over him who has the capacity to study but fails to do so; over him who has not the capacity for such study and yet engages upon it; and over him who rules the community with a high hand.

62b. A teacher should always be concise with his pupil, but never obscure.

63b. The teacher should repeat the lesson until the pupil has learned it.

64b. The maximum number of elementary pupils that should be placed under one teacher is twenty-five; if there are fifty an additional teacher must be provided; if there are forty, a senior student should be engaged to assist the teacher.

65b. Why was the city of Bethar great? Because there were four hundred schools in the town of Bethar, in each of which were four hundred teachers, and each teacher had four hundred pupils.

66b. A woman of sixty, like a girl of six, runs to the sound of the timbrel.

67b. A woman spins even while she talks.

68b. Women are compassionate.

69b. Women are light-minded.

70b. Ten measures of speech descended to the world; women took nine and men, one.

71b. The things for which a woman longs are adornments.

72b. It is not a woman's way to sit at home idle.

73b. A woman's thought is only for her appearance.

74b. The goose bends its head while walking, but its eyes wander.

75b. God endowed women with more intelligence than man.

76b. If your wife is short, bend down and whisper to her.

77b. When a man's first wife dies it is as though the Temple had been destroyed in his lifetime.

78b. Honor your wife and your life will be enriched.

79b. He who loves his wife as himself, honors her more than himself.

80b. A man's home is his wife.

81b. Descend a step in choosing a wife.

82b. Whoever marries a woman for her money will have disreputable children.

83b. A man should sell all he possesses, if necessary, to marry the daughter of a learned man.

84b. A man should spend less than his means on food and drink for himself, up to his means on his clothes and above his means on honoring his wife and children.

85b. A parent should never make distinctions between his children.

86b. A parent has no right to terrorize his children.

87b. When the majority declare a thing permitted it is permissible; when the majority declare against it it is forbidden.

88b. A man should not depart from the established practice: when Moses ascended Mount Sinai he did not eat; and when the ministering angels visited Abraham they partook of food.

89b. If you have entered a city conform to its laws.

90b. Man was created a single individual to teach the lesson that whoever destroys one life, Scripture ascribes it to him as though he had destroyed the whole world; and whoever saves one life, Scripture ascribes it to him as though he had saved the whole world.

91b. If need be, flay a carcass in the street and earn a living, and say not, "I am a great man and the work is below my dignity."

92b. Seven years the famine lasted, but it came not to the artisan's door.

93b. Great is the dignity of work for it honors the workmen.

94b. Idleness corrupts.

95b. Usurers are comparable to those who shed blood.

96b. A man should not eat his meal before giving food to his animals.

97b. Physical cleanliness leads to spiritual purity.

98b. Sixty runners ran but did not overtake the man who breakfasted.

99b. If the patient says he wants something and the physician says he may not have it, the former is listened to. For what reason? The heart knows its own bitterness.

100b. Heed your physician and you will not need him.

101b. When a person is brought before the tribunal (after death) the first question put to him is: "Have you dealt honestly with every man?"

ECCLESIASTICUS

Similar to The Proverbs of Solomon, in the Old Testament, is Ecclesiasticus, or The Wisdom of Jesus ben Sirach, in the Apocrypha. Who gathered this book of sayings, when and for what purpose, is given in a prologue which appears at the beginning of these sayings, written by an unknown author who lived over two thousand years ago. He wrote:

"This Jesus was the son of Sirach, and grandchild to Jesus of the same name with him; this man therefore lived in the latter times, after the people had been led away captive, and called home again, and almost after all the prophets. Now his grandfather Jesus, as he himself witnesses, was a man of great diligence and wisdom among the Hebrews, who did not only gather the grave and short sentences of wise men, that had been before him, but himself also uttered some of his own, full of much understanding and wisdom. When as therefore the first Jesus died, leaving the book almost perfected, Sirach his son receiving it after him left it to his own son Jesus, who, having gotten it into his hands, compiled it all orderly into one volume, and called it Wisdom, entitling it both by his own name, his father's name, and his grandfather's; alluring the hearer by the very name of Wisdom to have a greater love to the study of this book. It contains therefore wise sayings, dark sentences, and parables, and certain particular ancient godly stories of men who pleased God; also his prayer and song; moreover, what benefits God had vouchsafed his people, and what plagues he had heaped upon their enemies. This Jesus did imitate Solomon, and was no less famous for wisdom and learning, both being indeed a man of great learning, and so reputed also."

Sayings from
ECCLESIASTICUS

1c. All wisdom comes from the Lord. (1:1)

2c. Who can number the sand of the sea, and the drops of rain, and the days of eternity? (1:2)

3c. The fear of the Lord makes a merry heart, and gives joy, and gladness, and a long life. (1:12)

4c. If you desire wisdom, keep the commandments, and the Lord shall give it to you. (1:26)

5c. To fear the Lord is the beginning of wisdom. (1:14)

6c. Gold is tried in the fire, and acceptable men in the furnace of adversity. (2:5)

7c. Look at the generations of old and see; did ever any trust in the Lord, and was confounded? Or did any abide in his fear, and was forsaken? Or whom did he ever despise that called upon him? (2:10)

8c. Woe to fearful hearts, and faint hands, and the sinner that goes in two ways! (2:12)

9c. Woe to you who have lost patience! What will you do when the Lord shall visit you? (2:14)

10c. We will fall into the hands of the Lord, and not into the hands of men: for as his nature is, so is his mercy. (2:18)

11c. He who honors his father makes an atonement for his sins; and he who honors his mother is as one who lays up treasure. (3:3-4)

12c. He who honors his father shall have joy of his own children. (3:5)

13c. The greater you are, humble yourself the more, and you shall find favor before the Lord. (3:18)

14c. Many are in high place and of renown; but mysteries are revealed to the meek. (3:19)

15c. An obstinate heart shall be laden with sorrow. (3:27)

16c. Water will quench a flaming fire; and alms makes an atonement for sins. (3:30)

17c. Add not more trouble to a heart that is vexed; and defer not to give to him who is in need. (4:3)

18c. Make not a hungry soul sorrowful; neither provoke a man in his distress. (4:2)

19c. Deliver him who suffers wrong from the hand of the oppressor; and be not faint-hearted when you sit in judgment. (4:9)

20c. Wisdom exalts her children, and lays hold of those who seek her. (4:11)

21c. Observe the opportunity, and beware of evil; and be not ashamed when it concerns your soul. For there is a shame which brings sin; and there is a shame which is glory and grace. (4:20-21)

22c. Make not yourself an underling to a foolish man; neither accept the person of the mighty. (4:27)

23c. Strive for the truth to death, and the Lord will fight for you. (4:28)

24c. Be not hasty in speech, and in your deeds slack and remiss. (4:29)

25c. Let not your hand be stretched out to receive, and shut when you should repay. (4:31)

26c. Winnow not with every wind, and go not along every way. (5:9)

27c. If you have understanding, answer your neighbor; if not, lay your hand upon your mouth. (5:12)

28c. Sweet language will multiply friends; and a fair-speaking tongue will increase kind greetings. (6:5)

29c. Be in peace with many; nevertheless have but one counselor of a thousand. (6:6)

30c. If you would get a friend, prove him first, and be not hasty to credit him. (6:7)

31c. A faithful friend is a strong defence; and he who has found such a one has found a treasure. (6:14)

32c. My son, gather instruction from your youth up; so shall you find wisdom till your old age. (6:17)

33c. Do no evil, so shall no harm come to you. (7:1)

34c. My son, sow not upon the furrows of unrighteousness, and you shall not reap them seven-fold. (7:3)

35c. Laugh no man to scorn in the bitterness of his soul; for there is One who humbles and exalts. (7:11)

36c. Forego not a wise and good woman; for her grace is above gold. (7:19)

37c. Marry off your daughter, and so shall you have performed a weighty matter; but give her to a man of understanding. (7:25)

38c. Fail not to be with those who weep, and mourn with those who mourn. (7:34)

39c. Be not slow to visit the sick. (7:35)

40c. Whatever you take in hand, remember the end, and you shall never do amiss. (7:36)

41c. Rejoice not over your greatest enemy being dead, but remember that we all die. (8:7)

42c. Go not to law with a judge, for they will judge for him according to his honor. (8:14)

43c. Be not surety above your power: for if you are surety, take care to pay it. (8:13)

44c. Consult not with a fool, for he cannot keep counsel. (8:17)

45c. Open not your heart to every man, lest he requite you with a shrewd turn. (8:19)

46c. Many have been deceived by the beauty of a woman, for with it love is kindled like a fire. (9:8)

47c. Forsake not an old friend, for the new is not comparable to him; a new friend is like new wine; when it is old you shall drink it with pleasure. (9:10)

48c. Envy not the glory of a sinner: for you know not what shall be his end. (9:11)

49c. A man of an ill tongue is dangerous in his city; he who is rash in his talk shall be hated. (9:18)

50c. As the judge of the people is himself, so are his officers; and what manner of man the ruler of the city is, such are all those who dwell in it. (10:2)

51c. Who will justify him who sins against his own soul? And who will honor him who dishonors his own life? (10:29)

52c. The poor man is honored for his skill, and the rich man is honored for his riches. (10:30)

53c. The bee is little among such as fly, but her fruit is the chief of sweet things. (11:3)

54c. Boast not of your clothing and raiment, and exalt not yourself in the day of honor: for the works of the Lord are wonderful, and his works among men are hidden. (11:4)

55c. Blame not before you have examined the truth: understand first, and then rebuke. (11:7)

56c. Answer not before you have heard the cause. (11:18)

57c. Marvel not at the works of sinners; but trust in the Lord, and abide in your labor: for it is an easy thing in the sight of the Lord, on the sudden to make a poor man rich. (11:21)

58c. In the day of prosperity there is a forgetfulness of affliction; in the day of affliction there is no more remembrance of prosperity. (11:25)

59c. Bring not every man into your house: for the deceitful man has many plots. (11:29)

60c. A friend cannot be known in prosperity; an enemy cannot be hidden in adversity. (12:8)

61c. He who touches pitch shall be defiled by it. (13:1)

62c. The rich man has done wrong, and yet he threatens withal; the poor is wronged, and he must also entreat. (13:3)

63c. What fellowship has the wolf with the lamb? So the sinner with the godly. (13:17)

64c. The heart of a man changes his countenance, whether for good or evil. (13:25)

65c. Blessed is he whose conscience has not condemned him. (14:2)

66c. The envious man has a wicked eye. (14:8)

67c. Say not, "He has caused me to err"; for He has no need of the sinful man. (15:12)

68c. Before man is life and death; and whether or not he likes shall be given him. (15:17)

69c. He has commanded no man to do wickedly, neither has he given any man license to sin. (15:20)

70c. As His mercy is great, so is his correction also: he judges a man according to his works. (16:12)

71c. Make way for every work of mercy. (16:14)

72c. The number of a man's days at the most are a hundred years. As a drop of water to the sea, and a gravel-stone in comparison with the sand, so are a thousand years to the days of eternity. Therefore is God patient with them and pours forth His mercy upon them. (18:9-11)

73c. My son, do not blemish your good deeds, or use uncomfortable words when you give anything. Shall not the dew assuage the heat? So is a word better than a gift.

Lo, is not a word better than a gift? But both are with a gracious man. (18:15-17)

74c. When you have enough remember the time of hunger; and when you are rich, think upon poverty and need. (18:25)

75c. Be not made a beggar by banqueting upon borrowing. (18:33)

76c. Wine and women will make men of understanding fall away. (19:2)

77c. Whether it be to a friend or foe, talk not of other men's lives. (19:8)

78c. Admonish a friend: it may be he has not done it, and if he has done it, that he will do it no more. Admonish your friend: it may be he has not said it, and if he has, that he will not say it again. Admonish a friend: for many times it is a slander; and believe not every tale. (19:13-15)

79c. The knowledge of wickedness is not wisdom, neither at any time the counsel of sinners prudence. (19:22)

80c. There is a wicked man who hangs his head down sadly, but inwardly he is full of deceit. (19:26)

81c. A man's attire, and excessive laughter, and gait, show what he is. (19:30)

82c. It is much better to reprove, than to be angry secretly. (20:2)

83c. There is an abasement because of glory; and there is that which lifts up his head from a low estate. (20:11)

84c. To slip upon a pavement is better than to slip with the tongue. (20:18)

85c. A wise sentence shall be rejected when it comes out of a fool's mouth; for he will not speak it in due season. (20:20)

86c. A thief is better than a man who is accustomed to lie. (20:25)

87c. Wisdom that is hidden, and treasure that is hoarded, what profit is in them both? (20:30)

88c. Better is he who hides his folly than a man who hides his wisdom. (20:31)

89c. My son, you have sinned? Do so no more, but ask pardon for your former sins. (21:1)

90c. Flee from sin as from the face of a serpent, for if you come too near it it will bite you. (21:2)

91c. A prayer out of a poor man's mouth reaches to the ears of God, and his judgment comes speedily. (21:5)

92c. The heart of fools is in their mouth, but the mouth of the wise is in their heart. (21:26)

93c. Pales set on a high place will never stand against the wind: so a fearful heart in the imagination of a fool cannot stand against any fear. (22:18)

94c. Be faithful to your neighbor in his poverty, that you may rejoice in his prosperity. (22:23)

95c. I will not be ashamed to defend a friend; neither will I hide myself from him. (22:25)

96c. In three things I was beautified, and stood up beautiful both before God and men: the unity of brothers, the love of neighbors, a man and a wife that agree together. (25:1)

97c. If you have gathered nothing in your youth, how can you find anything in your old age? (25:3)

98c. Much experience is the crown of old men. (25:6)

99c. O how great is he who finds wisdom! Yet there is none above him who fears the Lord. But the love of the Lord surpasses all things for illumination: he who holds it, to what shall he be likened? (25:10-11)

100c. As the climbing of a sandy way to the feet of the aged, so is a wife full of words to a quiet man. (25:20)

101c. I had rather dwell with a lion and a dragon, than with a wicked woman. (25:16)

102c. There are three things that my heart fears, and of the fourth I was sore afraid: the slander of a city, and the gathering together of an unruly multitude, and a false accusation; all these are worse than death. But a grief and sorrow is a woman who is jealous over another woman, and a scourge of the tongue which communicates with all. (26:5-6)

103c. As the sun when it rises in high heaven, so is the beauty of a good wife in the ordering of her house. (26:16)

104c. As golden pillars upon sockets of silver, so are fair feet with a constant heart. (26:18)

105c. A merchant shall hardly keep himself from doing wrong; and a huckster shall not be freed from sin. (26:29)

106c. The furnace proves the potter's vessels; so the trial of man is in his reasoning. (27:5)

107c. Forgive your neighbor the hurt that he has done to

you, so shall your sins also be forgiven when you pray.
(28:2)

108c. One man bears hatred against another, and does he
seek pardon from the Lord? (28:3)

109c. The stroke of the whip makes marks in the flesh;
but the stroke of the tongue breaks the bones. (28:17)

110c. Many have fallen by the edge of the sword; but not
so many as have fallen by the tongue. (28:18)

111c. Lend to your neighbor in time of his need. (29:2)

112c. There is no riches above a sound body, and no joy
above the joy of the heart. (30:16)

113c. As a signet of emerald in a work of gold, so is the
melody of music with pleasant wine. (32:6)

114c. From that thing which is false what truth can
come? (34:4)

115c. Dreams have deceived many, and those have failed
who put their trust in them. (34:7)

116c. Mercy is seasonable in the time of affliction, as
clouds of rain in the time of drought. (35:20)

117c. As the palate tastes the different kinds of venison,
so does a heart of understanding false speeches. (36:19)

118c. The beauty of a woman cheers the countenance,
and a man loves nothing better. (36:22)

119c. Hide your counsel from such as envy you. (37:10)

120c. Let the counsel of your own heart stand, for there
is no man more faithful to you than it. For a man's mind
sometimes tells him more than seven watchmen who sit
above in a high tower. (37:13-14)

121c. The skill of the physician shall lift up his head, and he in the sight of great men he shall be admired. (38:3)

122c. The Lord has created medicines out of the earth, and he who is wise will not abhor them. (38:4)

123c. The wisdom of a learned man comes by opportunity of leisure. (38:24)

124c. Look upon the rainbow, and praise Him that made it. (43:11)

125c. Work your work betimes, and in his time he will give you his reward. (51:30)

The Sayings of

MOHAMMEDANISM

No one is a true believer until
he loves for his brother what he
loves for himself. *Hadith*

MOHAMMEDANISM

In the year 570 A.D., according to tradition, a boy was born in Mecca to a member of the Koreish tribe that ruled the city, and he was named Mohammed ibn Abdulla ibn Abd-al-Muttalib ib Hashim—known to us as Mohammed. A legend arose long after his death that when Mohammed was born the heavens celebrated with a wondrous display of falling stars and the mountains of the earth trembled and sang, "There is no god but Allah!" and the valleys answered, "And Mohammed is his Prophet!"

Mohammed, whose father died before his son was born, spent his early childhood with his grandfather Muttalib and, at the age of eight, when his grandfather died, he went to live with his uncle, Abu Talib. Early in his childhood young Mohammed learned from his grandfather and his uncle about the religion of his people, a confused accretion of superstitions which were encrusted upon the centuries-old beliefs: that the Arabs were the descendants of Ishmael, Abraham's first-born son; that Mecca was a sacred city because Adam settled there after his expulsion from Paradise; that on the center of the earth, the very spot where Adam had built his tent, now stood the sacred shrine, the *Kaaba;* that into the eastern corner of this shrine was set the Black Stone, called the Ruby of Heaven, which Adam had brought with him from the Garden of Eden; that near the *Kaaba* is the *Zemzem,* the Well of Ishmael, where the forefather of all Arabs was miraculously saved from death by thirst after he and his mother Hagar were driven out of Abraham's house by the jealous Sarah. He also learned of a great many gods, represented by idols, the chief of whom was one named Allah. These and a great many other beliefs Mohammed learned and accepted in his childhood.

As he grew up, he devoted himself to purely personal affairs. At the age of twenty-five he married a wealthy widow, Khadijah, who was fifteen years older than himself. Though polygamy was then the rule among the Arabs, Mohammed married no other woman as long as Khadijah lived; and they had one child, a daughter, whom they named Fatima.

Then, at the age of forty, Mohammed had a vision, in which Allah, through the Angel Gabriel, commanded him to abolish idolatry in his land and to bring divine order and discipline to his people inspired by the One God. "There is no god but Allah and Mohammed is the Prophet of Allah!" This was the cornerstone of the new faith Mohammed was to teach. After the first vision, Mohammed had many others. And he went out in search of disciples. The first three disciples of Mohammed were his wife Khadijah, and Ali, who was later to marry Fatima, and Abu Bakr, who was to become Mohammed's father-in-law after Khadijah's death. But Mohammed found great difficulty in gaining a following among his people in Mecca. For ten years he went about preaching, revealing his visions, asking the people to give up idolatry, to submit to the Will of Allah, *Islam,* and become true believers, *Muslims.* But in Mecca he gained more enemies than followers. Until one day some pilgrims from Yathrib, a city about 250 miles from Mecca, heard Mohammed preach and carried back with them the message of Islam. As Mohammed's popularity grew in Yathrib, the animosity against him rose in Mecca; and finally a plot was developed in Mecca to kill Mohammed. In the summer of 622, when Mohammed learned of the plot, he fled from

Mecca to Yathrib. The night of his flight, called *Hegira* (the Flight), is the most important date in the religion of Islam, and they calculate time from A.H., *Anno Hegira*, the Year of the Flight. In Yathrib (now called the City of the Prophet, or Medina) Mohammed established his teachings. And in his teachings he retained as basic the concept that Mecca was a holy city to which each Muslim must, if possible, make at least one pilgrimage during his lifetime. Eight years after his flight (630 A.D.), Mohammed returned to his birthplace with an army of 10,000 to depose all idols and to place the city under Islam.

On June 8, 632 A.D. (10 A.H.) Mohammed died. Immediately his followers began collecting all the revelations of the prophet, as written down by his scribe and adopted son, Zeid ibn Thabit; and in 30 A.H., under Caliph Othman, the work was completed, consisting of 114 chapters, each representing one or more revelations, and arranged (with the exception of the first) according to length, from the longest to the shortest, regardless of chronology in the sequence of the revelations. The completed work is known as the *Koran,* which is Arabic for the Reading. And at the same time that the followers of Mohammed preserved their sacred scriptures, they started out to bring their religion to the attention of the entire world.

Within one century after Mohammed's death, his followers conquered Persia, Syria, Palestine, Egypt, North Africa, Spain and reached deep into France. The reasons for their phenomenal success are to be found more in the historical and economic circumstances of that time in those countries than in the irresistible persuasion of Islam.

Today every seventh person in the world is a Mohammedan or, as they prefer to be known, a Muslim. It is no longer a religion of Arabs only, for its followers are to be found in great numbers in China, Pakistan, Iran, Turkey, Russia and many other countries. They are divided into two main sects: the Sunnites and the Shi'ites. The split originally took place over the Caliphate, or the succession to Mohammed; the Sunnites claiming that the caliph must be chosen by the disciples and followers of Islam, while the Shi'ites claimed that the succession was inherited by Ali, Mohammed's son-in-law and by Husain, Ali's son. In time differences of ritual and doctrine also developed. The vast majority of Muslims today are Sunnites. Each of these sects produced denominations, some of which attracted wide attention. Such was the nineteenth-century movement of *Babism*, an outgrowth of the Shi'ites, which is of interest to us because it in turn produced *Bahaism*, which has found a following in the United States.

Whatever their differences, all branches of Islam accept the Koran as their sacred scriptures. To the Koran has been added a vast collection of traditional sayings, known as the Table Talk of Mohammed, or *Hadith*, covering the relationship of man with his fellowman—from abstinence, and the treatment of animals, to man's attitude toward women, in particular, and the world, in general; and man's relation to his God. There are some fifteen hundred collections of *Hadith*, of which four have been accepted, and which might be compared to the Apocrypha in the Judaic and Christian scriptures; whereas the others are Pseudepigraphic.

The sayings from the Koran are the precepts for all Muslims. The sayings from the Table Talk of Mohammed represent a code for daily living and presuppose the acceptance of the tenets of the Koran. The Muslim, the True Believer, begins with the Koran, then seeks guidance in the words of the prophet as given in the *Hadith*.

The Muslim sayings underscore these simple basic tenets, repeated with ingenious variation: Actions are to be judged by their intentions. No man is a True Believer unless he desires for his brothers what he desires for himself. Indulgence in gluttony and drink kills the heart. God cares little about the man who fasts and does not abandon lying and calumny. Self-torment is forbidden; if God considers a man deserving of punishment, He will know how to provide it. There is no monasticism in Islam. It is indispensable for every Muslim to give alms and to do acts of charity. These, and the Five Pillars of the Faith, are basically the foundation of Islam.

There are several English translations of the Koran, but the verse numbers do not always correspond in all of them. The *Hadith* sayings included here were all taken from *The Sayings of Muhammed* by Allama Sir Abdullah Al-Manum Al-Suhrawardy, and published in the Wisdom of the East series in London. At the end of each saying the numbers in parenthesis correspond to the numbers in *The Sayings of Muhammed*.

The Sayings of the
KORAN

1. Islam rests on five pillars: the recital of the *Kalima* (the confession: "There is but one God and Mohammed is his Prophet"); the five daily periods of prayer; the practice of charity; the fast during the month of Ramadan; and the pilgrimage to Mecca.

2. This is the Essence of the Koran: The seven most often repeated verses.
> ("Praise be to Allah, Lord of the Worlds,
> The Beneficent, the Merciful,
> Owner of the Day of Judgment,
> You we worship and of You we ask for help;
> Show us the straight path,
> The path of those whom You have favored,
> And not of those who deserve Your anger
> and have gone astray.")

3. O People! Serve Allah who created you and those who went before you. He made the earth as your resting place and the sky as your canopy; and he sends down rain from heaven to bring forth fruit with which to sustain you. As long as you know this, set up no rivals to Allah! (2:19-20)

4. Confound not truth with falsehood; nor knowingly conceal the truth. (2:39)

5. Will you order men to be pious and yourself forget it? (2:41)

6. Those who have faith and do good works are the rightful owners of the Garden (of Eden) and will dwell in it. (2:76)

7. Whatever good you do for others, you send it before your own souls and shall find it with Allah who sees all you do. (2:104)

8. Allah is in the east and Allah is in the west; wherever you turn there is Allah's face. (2:109)

9. To Allah belong the east and the west, and He guides whom he wills to the straight path. (2:136)

10. In the alternation of day and night, in the rains from heaven that come to quicken the parched earth, in the shifting winds, and in the clouds pressed into service between heaven and earth, there are signs enough of Allah's rule for people who have understanding. (2:159)

11. When misfortune strikes, say, "Verily we all come from Allah and to Allah we must return." (2:150)

12. Allah loves all those who do good. (2:191)

13. Fight in the way of Allah with those who fight you, but you do not begin the hostilities; for Allah does not love aggressors. (2:186)

14. Slay your enemies and drive them out from where they drove you out; for sedition is worse than slaughter. (2:187)

15. Allah wishes your ease not your discomfort. (2:179)

16. The righteous are not those who turn their heads to the east or the west, but those who believe in Allah and the angels and the Scriptures and the Prophets, and who

give of their wealth to their kin, the orphan, the needy and the wayfarer. (2:172)

17. Allah is with those who patiently endure. (2:148)

18. Whatever good you do, Allah knows it. (2:211)

19. When people ask what they should spend in charity, say, "All that you have left over above your needs." (2:216)

20. There is no compulsion in religion. (2:257)

21. If you give alms publicly, it is well; but it is better to give them secretly. Allah knows what you do. (2:273)

22. Wrong not and you will not be wronged. (2:279)

23. Allah will not burden any soul beyond its endurance. (2:286)

24. Those who believe (what Mohammed revealed), and those who are Jews, Christian, Sabeans or whoever believes in Allah and the Day of Judgment, they shall have their reward and there is no fear nor grief for them. (2:59)

25. Pleasant for mankind is the love of women and children, and the joy of gold and silver, and well-bred horses, and cattle, and land. But Allah, with him is the best resort. (3:12-14)

26. The true religion in Allah's sight is Islam. (3:17)

27. Every soul will be rewarded according to its merit. (3:182)

28. Do not pray when you are drunk, until you know what you utter. (4:43)

29. Whatever good befalls a man, it is from Allah; whatever ill befalls a man, it is his own doing. (4:79)

30. He who slays one human being, it is as if he had slain all mankind; he who saves one human being, it is as if he had saved all mankind. (5:35)

31. If Allah had wished He would have made all men alike; but He wished to test you by what he gave to each of you. (5:53)

32. O you who believe! Take not a Jew or a Christian as your friend. They are each other's friend. Anyone who takes them for his friend he is surely one of them. (5:56)

33. Not a leaf falls but Allah knows it. (6:59)

34. These are the Commandments binding on you:
    1. Ascribe nothing as partner to Allah;
    2. Be good to your parents;
    3. Slay not your children because of poverty—Allah will provide for them and for you;
    4. Come not near polluted things, open or concealed;
    5. Slay no one, except in a just cause;
    6. Approach not the property of an orphan save to improve it, until he comes of age;
    7. Give full measure and a just balance;
    8. In judgment observe justice, even in the affairs of a kinsman;
    9. Fulfill your covenant with Allah; and
    10. Follow no other paths, lest you depart from Allah's path. (6:152-154)

35. Those who deny Revelation shall not enter Paradise until the camel goes through the eye of a needle. (7:38)

36. Your wealth and your children are but a temptation. (8:28)

37. Apart from Allah you have neither friend nor helper. (9:11)

38. Every nation has its prophet; every nation has its time. (10:48)

39. The Lord said to the bee: "Choose your habitation in the hills and build your hives in the trees; eat of every fruit and walk in the path of the Lord." And the bees out of their body produce honey which is a cure for men. Verily these are signs for men to reflect upon. (16:70)

40. If you do good, you do good for your own souls; if you do evil, you do it to yourselves. (17:7)

41. Man prays for evil and he prays for good; for man is ever hasty. (17:12)

42. No soul shall bear the burden of another. (17:16)

43. The wastrel is the devil's brother. (17:29)

44. Let not your hand be tied to your neck; nor yet open it too freely, lest you yourself be reduced to beggary. (17:31)

45. He who is blind in this life will be blind in the Hereafter. (17:74)

46. Truth has come and falsehood has vanished; for falsehood cannot endure. (17:83)

47. God is witness enough between you and me. (17:98)

48. God will increase the guidance of those already guided. (19:78)

49. Every soul must taste of death. (21:36)

50. A day with Allah is as a thousand of man's years. (22:46)

51. Kings, when they enter a city, despoil it. (27:54)

52. He who takes guidance from others than Allah might be likened to the spider building his house; surely the frailest of all houses is the house of the spider. (29:40)

53. Our God and your God are One, and to Him are we self-surrendered (Muslims). (29:45)

54. Were all the trees on earth pens, and the sea with seven more seas to increase it, ink, they would still not suffice for the words of Allah. (31:26)

55. Repay evil with good and, lo, he between whom and you there was enmity will become your warm friend. (41:34)

56. They speak with their tongues what is not in their hearts. (48:11)

57. All believers are brothers. (49:10)

58. Can the reward of goodness be aught but goodness? (55:60)

59. Wait for us that we may kindle our candle by yours. (57:13)

60. Those who give in charity have lent to Allah a goodly loan. (57:18)

61. Three persons speak not privately together, but He is their fourth. (58:8)

62. Do no favors in order that you may later receive them in return with increase. (74:6)

63. Man loves the transitory and neglects the eternal. (75:20)

64. To him who is covetous and bent on riches and who calls good a lie, to him will the path of distress be made easy. (92:8-10)

65. Did He not find you an orphan and gave you a home? Did He not find you lost and showed you the way? Did He not find you needy and enriched you? (93:6-8)

66. On that day shall men behold their works: and whoever had wrought an ant's weight in good shall behold it; and whoever had wrought an ant's weight in evil shall behold it. (99:6)

67. As the day declines, man is in a state of loss, save those who have faith and do good works. (103:1-3)

68. The slanderer who has gathered wealth thinks that his wealth will make him immortal. (104:1-3)

The Sayings of

MOHAMMED

(as found in the *Hadith*)

1a. Actions will be judged by their intentions. (1)

2a. The proof of a Muslim's sincerity is that he pays no attention to matters which are not his business. (2)

3a. No man can be considered a True Believer who does not seek for his brother what he seeks for himself. (3)

4a. What is lawful is clear, and what is unlawful is clear; but there are doubtful matters between the two from which it is well to abstain. (4)

5a. God cares not for the keeper of the fast who does not abandon lying and slander. (6)

6a. There is no monasticism in Islam. (10)

7a. Faith leaves the man who commits adultery; when he repents his evil ways, Faith will return to him. (14)

8a. The eye and the tongue can commit adultery. (15)

9a. There is nothing which God abhors more than adultery. (16)

10a. To honor an old man is to show respect for God. (19)

11a. The best of charity is that which the right hand gives and the left hand does not know it. (20)

12a. Almsgiving is the duty of every Muslim. (22)

13a. There are seven kinds of people whom God will draw into His own shadow on the Judgment Day; and one of these will be the men who have given charity and concealed it, so that his left hand did not know what his right hand did. (23)

14a. The angels asked: "O God, is there anything You have created stronger than rock?" God said: "Yes, iron is stronger than rock, for iron breaks it." The angels asked: "O Lord! Is there anything stronger than iron?" God said: "Yes, fire is stronger than iron; for fire melts it." The angels asked: "Is there anything stronger than fire?" God answered: "Yes, water is stronger than fire; for water extinguishes fire." The angels asked: "Is there anything stronger than water?" God said: "Yes, wind is stronger than water; for wind can put water in motion." Then the angels asked: "O Defender! Is there anything stronger than wind?" God said: "Yes, those who give charity and their left hand does not know what their right hand does, they overcome all." (26)

15a. Charity begins with one's own family, if they are poor. (29)

16a. An adulteress passed by a dog at a well, and the dog held out his tongue for thirst; and the woman took off her shoe and tied it to the end of her garment and drew water for the dog to drink; and for that act she was forgiven her sin. (31)

17a. Mohammed said, "Verily there is a heavenly reward for every act of kindness to a living animal." (33)

18a. Slander destroys the good of ablution and fasting. (36)

19a. The person who has one atom of pride in his heart will not enter Paradise. (37)

20a. The man who begs to increase his property, God will diminish it. (38)

21a. Whoever has food for a day, it is prohibited for him to beg. (42)

22a. Charity is the duty of every Muslim. If he has nothing to give, let him do a good deed or abstain from doing an evil one. (48)

23a. The best of God's servants are those who, when seen, remind one of God; and the worst of God's servants are those who search for the defects of the just. (49)

24a. Every good act is charity. (51)

25a. Modesty and charity are parts of faith. (55)

26a. "Do not exceed bounds in praising me, as the Christians do in praising Jesus, the son of Mary, by calling him God and the Son of God; I am only the Lord's servant; then call me the servant of God and His messenger." (57)

27a. God is pure and He loves purity and cleanliness. (60)

28a. A man asked Mohammed how to tell when one is truly faithful, and he replied: "If you derive pleasure from the good which you do and are grieved by the evil which you commit, then you are a true believer." (67)

29a. Riches do not come from an abundance of goods but from a contented mind. (69)

30a. Look down to those who are not as well-off as you are, so that you may not hold God's benefits in contempt. (71)

31a. God loves those who are content. (72)

32a. A man cannot become a Muslim until his heart and tongue are so. (75)

33a. Mohammed was asked for advice, and he said, "Be not angry." (80)

34a. He is not strong who throws others down; but he is strong who controls his anger. (82)

35a. Humility and courtesy are acts of piety. (84)

36a. A guest should not stay so long as to inconvenience his host. (86)

37a. No father can give his child anything better than good manners. (87)

38a. Meekness and modesty are two branches of the Faith. (94)

39a. When three persons are together, two of them must not whisper to each other without letting the third hear, because it would hurt him. (95)

40a. These are the greatest crimes: to seek after another god than God; to vex one's father and mother; to commit murder; to commit suicide; and to swear to a lie. (96)

41a. Never speak ill of the dead. (101)

42a. Wish not for death nor pray for it before your time comes; for in the increase of a Muslim's life there is an increase in good deeds. (103)

43a. Death is a blessing to a Muslim. (107)

44a. There are two things disliked by men: one of them is death, and the other is a scarcity of money. (108)

45a. The grave is the first station in the journey to eternity. (109)

46a. Death is a chasm that separates friend from friend. (110)

47a. Sleep is brother to death. (111)

48a. God is pleased with deliberation in undertakings. (116)

49a. He is the most perfect Muslim whose disposition is best liked by his own family. (118)

50a. Two qualities are not tolerated in any Muslim: avarice, and a bad disposition. (123)

51a. Mankind will not go astray after having found the right road, unless from disputation. (124)

52a. Divorce is lawful, but disliked by God. (126)

53a. Happy is the Muslim, for if good befalls him, he thanks God; and if evil befalls him, he praises God and bears his misfortune patiently. (130)

54a. Mohammed said: "Keep your heart from morning till night and from night till morning free of malice toward anyone. This is one of my laws; and he who loves my laws loves me." (132)

55a. Do not drink wine, for it is the root of all evil; abstain from vice; and cherish your children. (136)

56a. Love him who loves God; hate him who hates God;

and keep your tongue employed in repeating the name of God. (138)

57a. Do unto all men as you would wish to have done unto you; and reject for others what you would reject for yourselves. (138a)

58a. Even he who makes progress daily is still far off from the ideal. (139)

59a. Speak to men according to their mental capacities; for if you speak to men of things they cannot understand, they may fall into error. (143)

60a. Verily your deed will be brought back to you, as if you yourself meted out your own punishment. (145)

61a. Adore God as if you could see Him; for although you cannot see Him, He can see you. (146)

62a. A true Muslim is thankful to God in prosperity, and resigned to His will in adversity. (153)

63a. He is true who protects his brothers both present and absent. (156)

64a. No man is a true believer who does not desire for his brother that which he desires for himself. (164)

65a. It is unworthy of a Muslim to injure another's reputation, to curse anyone, to abuse anyone, and to talk vainly. (169)

66a. It is better to sit alone than in the company of evil. (170)

67a. Refrain from speaking of the vices of mankind which you know are in yourself. (172)

68a. Guard yourself in six things: When you speak, speak the truth; keep your promise; discharge your trust; be chaste in all actions; withold your hand from striking; and from taking that which is unlawful and bad. (173)

69a. Each of you is a mirror of his brother: then if you see a vice in your brother you must tell him to get rid of it. (178)

70a. He is not a perfect Muslim who eats his fill and lets his neighbor go hungry. (179)

71a. Do not say, "To those who are good to me, I will be good; and those who oppress me, I will oppress." But rather, be good to those who are good to you; and those who oppress you, do not oppress. (181)

72a. Mohammed said: "Desire not the world, and God will love you; and desire not what other men have, and they will love you." (182)

73a. Some eloquence is like magic. (187)

74a. Keep far from envy; for as fire burns wood, so envy consumes good actions. (189)

75a. There is no physician like experience. (190)

76a. God is gentle and loves gentleness. (198)

77a. God is One and therefore likes unity. (205)

78a. Do you love your Creator? Then love your fellow-beings first. (208)

79a. God said: "Verily My compassion overcomes My wrath!" (210)

80a. God's kindness toward His creatures is greater than a mother's toward her babe. (212)

81a. Trust in God, but tie your camel. (214)

82a. God is not merciful to him who is not merciful to men. (215)

83a. Be persistent in good action. (218)

84a. Hell is veiled in delights; Heaven, in hardships and miseries. (221)

85a. Heaven lies at the feet of mothers. (222)

86a. Paradise is nearer to you than the thongs of your sandals. (224)

87a. Paradise is not for him who reproaches others with any favor he does for them. (227)

88a. Whoever is humble to men for God's sake, him God will exalt. (237)

89a. Religion is like rain: when it falls on good soil, it causes fresh grass to grow. (240)

90a. Mohammed was asked: "What is the essence of Islam?" And he replied: "Purity of speech, and charity." (243)

91a. Every child is born with a natural inclination toward Islam. It is his parents who make a Jew, a Christian, or a Magian out of him. (244)

92a. Do you know who undermines the foundations of Islam? The errors of the learned; the disputations of the hypocrites; and the orders of the kings who have lost the road. (245)

93a. He who helps his fellowmen in the hour of need, him will God help in the Day of Travail. (248)

94a. All God's creatures are His family; and he is most beloved of God who does most good to His creatures. (251)

95a. Kindness is the mark of faith; whoever has no kindness can have no faith. (254)

96a. God has not made it lawful for you to enter the houses of the People of the Book (Jews and Christians) without their permission; nor has He made it lawful for you to beat their women or eat their fruits. (256)

97a. The *Koran* was sent down in seven dialects; and in every one of its sentences there is an outer and inner meaning. (257)

98a. Pray to God morning and evening, and employ the day in your useful avocation. (260)

99a. He who is fit and able to work for himself or others and does not, God is not gracious to him. (262)

100a. Those who earn an honest living are beloved of God. (263)

101a. God is gracious to him who earns his living by his own labor. (264)

102a. Give the laborer his wages before his perspiration is dry. (266)

103a. He dies not who gives his life to learning. (267)

104a. He who honors the learned, honors Me. (268)

105a. The worst of men is a bad learned man; and the best of men is a good learned man. (269)

106a. God takes away knowledge from his servants by

taking away the learned; so that when no learned men remain, the ignorant are placed at the head of affairs. (270)

107a. An hour of contemplation is worth a year of adoration. (271)

108a. Go in quest of knowledge even to the ends of the earth. (273)

109a. Seek knowledge from the cradle to the grave. (274)

110a. It is better to teach knowledge one hour than to pray all night. (277)

111a. Whoever seeks knowledge and finds it will get two rewards: one for seeking, and the other for finding. If he does not find it, he still has one reward. (278)

112a. One learned man is harder on the devil than a thousand ignorant worshipers. (280)

113a. He who knows his own self, knows God. (282)

114a. The ink of the scholar is holier than the blood of the martyr. (285)

115a. God has many treasuries beneath his throne, and the keys thereof are the tongues of the poets. (288)

116a. Acquire knowledge: it enables its possessor to distinguish right from wrong. (290)

117a. With knowledge man rises to the heights of goodness and a noble position, associates with the sovereigns of this world; and attains the perfection of happiness in the next world. (291)

118a. Who are the learned? They who practice what they know. (294)

119a. As a man grows, two things grow with him: love of wealth and love of longevity. (295)

120a. All should marry who can. (297)

121a. Whatever mishap befalls you, it is on account of something which you have done. (300)

122a. True modesty is the source of all virtues. (302)

123a. All kinds of modesty are best. (305)

124a. Monopoly is unlawful in Islam. (306)

125a. Mohammed said: "My sayings do not abrogate the word of God, but the word of God can abrogate my sayings." (314)

126a. Once Mohammed was distributing food in Ji'ranah, and behold, a woman came close to him and he spread his garment for her to sit upon. When the people asked who she was, they were told, "This was his nurse." (318)

127a. Mohammed was asked to curse the infidels, and he answered: "I was not sent to curse the infidels but to have mercy on mankind." (325)

128a. Shall I tell you what are better acts than fasting, charity and prayers? Making peace between enemies are such acts; for enmity and malice tear up the heavenly rewards by the roots. (340)

129a. Poverty may well become the cause of infidelity. (346)

130a. The key to Paradise is prayer; and the key to prayer is ablution. (354)

131a. Mohammed said: "God is Beauty and delights in

the beautiful; but pride in it causes man to be held in contempt." (357)

132a. Everyone is divinely furthered according to his character. (359)

133a. Every human being has two inclinations: one prompting him to do good, and the other impelling him to do evil. He who asks the help of God to contend with evil will receive assistance. (361)

134a. Men will love liars to the end of the world, and will relate such stories as neither you nor your fathers ever heard. (364)

135a. Religion is admonition; and it requires of you to be pure. (371)

136a. God has created nothing better than Reason. (372)

137a. When your friend dies, mention not his vices. (373)

138a. God's favor does not descend on the family in which relatives are deserted. (375)

139a. The duty of a junior to a senior brother is that of a child to his father. (378)

140a. He who repents sincerely is as one who committed no sin. (381)

141a. It is difficult for a man laden with riches to climb the steep path that leads to bliss. (384)

142a. Wealth, properly employed, is a blessing; and one may lawfully endeavor to increase it by honest means. (386)

143a. To those of your servants who please you give to eat what you eat yourself, and clothe them as yourself;

but those who do not please you, part with them, but do not punish God's creatures. (389)

144a. He will not enter Paradise who behaves ill toward his servants. (390)

145a. On the Day of Judgment God will say: "O children of Adam! I was sick and you did not visit me. I asked you for food, and you did not give it to Me." And they replied: "You are the Lord of the Universe, how could you be sick and how could we visit you? And how could we give you food, since you are free from hunger and thirst?" And God said: "Such and such a one was sick, and you did not visit him; such and such a one asked you for bread and you did not give it to him." (397)

146a. He is true in the truest sense of the word who is true in word, in thought, and in deed. (401)

147a. It is not worthy of a speaker of truth to curse the people. (403)

148a. Say what is true, even if it is bitter and displeasing to you. (405)

149a. The taker of usury, and the giver of it, and writer of the papers and witness to it, are equal in crime. (408)

150a. Admonish your wives with kindness. (411)

151a. You must not beat your wife as you would a slave. (413)

152a. He is the most perfect Muslim whose disposition is best; and the best of you are those who behave best to their wives. (417)

153a. A virtuous wife is a man's greatest treasure. (418)

154a. The world and all things in it are valuable; but the most valuable of all is a virtuous woman. (420)

155a. God enjoins you to treat women well, for they are your mothers, daughters, and aunts. (430)

156a. The rights of women are sacred. (431)

157a. The love of the world is the root of all evil. (433)

158a. This world is a prison for the Faithful, but a Paradise for unbelievers. (434)

159a. Be in this world like a traveler, or like a passer on, and reckon yourself as of the dead. (438)

The Sayings of

SHINTOISM

One should not be mindful of
suffering in his own life and
unmindful of suffering in the
lives of others.
(*From the Sacred Text of Kyo Koyen*)

SHINTOISM

There are some religions which have become histori-
cally associated with a particular people and a particular
land, or even a particular city, though the ethical principles of the religion itself are universal. And there is one,
among the living religions, which is predominantly nationalistic. This religion, native to Japan, is called *Kami-no-
Michi*, though it is best known by its Chinese name,
Shinto, or *Shen-Tao*, which means The Way of the Good
Spirits. In Shinto theology and patriotism are so deeply
intertwined that some scholars have debated whether it is
a religion or a cult of patriotism.

But by definition Shinto belongs among the religions,
since it gives a theory of creation and a deistic explanation
of its origins.

According to Shinto, there are many gods in heaven.
Two of these gods, Izanagi the Positive (Male) and
Izanami the Negative (Female) created the eight Japanese Islands from which the earth was henceforth to be
ruled. These islands were inhabited by the offspring of
Izanagi and Izanami, the most illustrious of which was the
Sun Goddess, Amaterasu-Omi-Kami. And it was her
grandson, Jimmu Tenno, who became the first emperor of
Japan and, by implication, of the world. This happened
in the year 660 B.C., which is the year one of the Japanese
era. Jimmu Tenno, offspring of the Sun Goddess, and his
descendants after him, were chosen in that year as the
divine representatives. They were empowered to rule the
earth and all that was on it, and their subjects were to

worship them as they would worship the Sun Goddess, Amaterasu-Omi-Kami. The person of the Mikado was sacred; and it was the sacred duty of every subject to give their devotion and loyalty to him. This, the essence of Shintoism, when amplified and recorded, filled a number of volumes.

The most important of the Shinto sacred scriptures are *Ko-ji-ki,* or The Records of Ancient Matters, compiled in 712 A.D., and *Nihongi,* or The Chronicles of Japan, added eight years later. These two books give the legends of Creation, the Divine Origin of the Mikado and the genealogies of the emperors since Jimmu Tenno, who, when he first ascended the Japanese throne, promised his people that "hereafter the imperial rule shall be extended so as to embrace the entire world, and the universe shall be covered so as to form a single roof." And from the beginning, and until very recent times, it was the heavenly mission of the Mikado and his loyal subjects to conquer the world and bring all people under the divine shelter of "a single roof."

The religion of Shinto has gone through a number of reformations. About the middle of the sixth century A.D., the teachings of Buddhism and Confucianism were brought from China and gave rise to great changes in the teachings and beliefs of Shinto. Many sects arose. But most of them, whatever their sectarian differences, retained the central conviction that weds Japanese religious creed and ritual with the Japanese emperor.

In modern times, when Japan began to exert great influence in Asia outside her own borders, Shintoism supplied the conviction that their conquests were justified from heaven and that they were only fulfilling heaven's will to bring the whole world under "a single roof."

Shintoism has developed a lofty, if narrowly nationalistic, ethic. Since Shintoists must worship their emperor, who is of divine origin, it follows that they must also try to emulate him and strive to attain his perfections. Foremost among the emperor's perfections are: purity, sincerity, truthfulness and courage. These perfections, spelled out in concrete and daily application, became the essence of Shinto teachings. The abolition of emperor-worship in 1945, when Japan was defeated in World War II, did not in any way affect the beliefs and the ritual practices of their centuries-old religion; and Shintoism continues to thrive in that land.

A group of laws or principles, propounded by the Imperial Prince, are given in Chapter XXII of *Nihongi*. And from these the following precepts and maxims were culled. To these were added proverbs from the text of *Kurozumi Kyo* and *Konko Kyo*.

Sayings from the Chronicles of JAPAN

1. Harmony is to be valued, and an avoidance of wanton opposition to be honored.

2. All men are influenced by class feeling, and there are few who are intelligent.

3. When those above are in harmony and those below are friendly, and there is concord in the discussion of business, right views gain acceptance.

4. Few men are utterly bad.

5. When you receive the Imperial commands, fail not scrupulously to obey them.

6. The lord is Heaven; the vassal is Earth. Heaven overspreads and the Earth upbears. If the Earth attempted to overspread, Heaven would simply fall in ruin.

7. Ministers and functionaries should make decorous behavior their leading principle. If the superiors do not behave with decorum, the inferiors will be disorderly; and if the inferiors are disorderly, there are bound to be offenses.

8. Of complaints by the people there are a thousand in one day. If in one day there are so many, how many will there be in the course of several years?

9. If a judge makes gain his motive, and hears cases with

a view of receiving bribes, the plaints of the poor will resemble water cast upon a stone.

10. Chastise that which is evil and encourage that which is good: this was an excellent rule of antiquity.

11. Conceal not the good qualities of others; and fail not to correct that which is wrong when you see it.

12. Flatterers and deceivers are sharp weapons for the overthrow of the State, and pointed swords for the destruction of the people.

13. Sycophants are fond of relating to their superiors the errors of their inferiors; and to their inferiors they criticize the faults of their superiors. From such, civil disturbances arise.

14. When wise men are entrusted with office, the sound of praise arises.

15. In this world few are born with knowledge: wisdom is the product of earnest meditation.

16. In all things, whether great or small, find the right man, and they will be well managed.

17. The wise sovereigns of antiquity sought men to fill the office, and not the office for sake of the man.

18. The business of the State does not admit of laxity, and the whole day is hardly enough for its accomplishment.

19. Good faith is the foundation of right.

20. If the lord and vassal observe good faith one with another, what is there which they cannot accomplish?

21. Let us cease from wrath and refrain from angry looks.

22. Be not resentful when others differ with you.

23. All men have hearts, and each heart has its own leaning.

24. We are not unquestionably sages; they are not unquestionably fools.

25. How can one lay down a rule by which to distinguish right from wrong?

26. Though we alone may be in the right, let us follow the multitude and act like them.

27. Give clear appreciation to merit and demerit, and deal out to each its sure reward or punishment.

28. There can be no two lords in a country; the people cannot be asked to serve two masters.

29. If we envy others, they in turn will envy us: the evil of envy knows no limit.

30. If others excel us in intelligence, it gives us no pleasure.

31. It is not until after a lapse of five hundred years that we meet with a wise man; and after a thousand years that we obtain a sage.

32. To turn away from that which is private, and to set our faces toward that which is public—that is the duty of a Minister.

33. Decisions on important matters should not be made by one person alone.

45. One should not be mindful of suffering in his own
and unmindful of suffering in the lives of others.

46. Your body is not for you to do as you please.

with such gratitude as

47. Faith is the mind that catches the things that are
hidden and lets the things that are apparent have care of
themselves.

48. Where the heart of Amaterasu-Oho-Kami, God of the

death.

Sayings from the
KUROZUMI KYO
and KONKO KYO

34. Both heaven and hell come from one's own heart.

35. If in one's heart one is a serpent, then one becomes a
serpent.

36. All men are brothers; all receive the blessings of the
same heaven.

37. Free yourself from doubt and you will find your life
quickened in the midst of the goodness of God.

38. With God there is neither day nor night, neither far
nor near.

39. Sincerity is the witness of Truth.

40. With sincerity there is no such thing as failure.

41. Faith is just like filial obedience to parents.

42. When prayer fails to help you accomplish your purpose, know that something is lacking in your sincerity.

43. Bring not suffering upon yourself by indulging in selfishness.

44. Do not profess love with your lips while you harbor
hatred in your heart.

255

45. One should not be mindful of suffering in his own life and unmindful of suffering in the lives of others.

46. Your body is not for your own freedom.

47. Nothing in all the world calls forth such gratitude as sincerity.

48. Happy is the man who cultivates the things that are hidden and lets the things that are apparent take care of themselves.

49. When the heart of Amaterasu-Omi-Kami and our hearts are undivided, then there is no such thing as death.

50. In all the world there is no such thing as a stranger.

The Sayings of

TAOISM

He is fit to govern who loves
all people as he loves himself.
(*Tao-Te-King, 13*)

THE TAO-TE-KING

The *Tao-Te-King,* a collection of eighty-one fairly brief poems, is the sacred scriptures of the Taoists, and is by far the shortest of all the Bibles of the world's religions. It is a short book but a puzzling one. For it contains many mystic and paradoxical concepts. And it literally defies elucidation. Toward the end of this little book, he who might attempt to make the opaque transparent, or even translucent, is sharply warned: "They who tell do not know; they who know do not tell" anything about *Tao.* Of course this warning did not deter devout followers from "telling" voluminously what *Tao* and the *Tao-Te-King* mean. The cryptic little book of loosely knit poems became the subject of a library of commentary and interpretation. But in the end nothing really became clearer. The mystic concepts remain obscure, the paradoxes remain unresolved. The basic residue for the non-follower of *Tao* is still to be found in the sayings as they appear in the *Tao-Te-King.* Collectively they underscore the ethical concepts prescribed for the Taoist. And though one perceives in them an affinity with concepts found in other religions, particularly Buddhism, they have their own flavor because they are founded on a different set of premises.

Here the *Tao-Te-King* is presented in the form of a sequence of sayings, and the numbers in parentheses refer to the numbered poems in the order in which they appear.

The Sayings of the
TAO-TE-KING

1. The way which has a name is not the Eternal Way. (1)

2. Nameless are the origins of all creation. (1)

3. All things have a mother, and she has a name. (1)

4. The secret waits for the proper insight. (1)

5. Those who are motivated by desire see only the outer shell of things. (1)

6. Good implies the idea of evil; and beauty implies the idea of ugliness. (2)

7. Is and Is-Not come together. (2)

8. Hard and easy complement each other. (2)

9. Long and short, high and low, can be known only by comparison. (2)

10. Before and after is a matter of sequence. (2)

11. The wise man does not teach by words but by deeds. (2)

12. The wise man takes no credit for his wisdom; but credit never leaves him. (2)

13. Where promotion is not prized, people will not contend for it. (3)

14. Where people would not prize things highly simply because they are hard to get, thieving would cease. (3)

15. The wise ruler empties people's minds and fills their bellies; he weakens their ambitions and strengthens their bones. He practices inaction, and nothing remains ungoverned. (3)

16. The Way is like an empty vessel which is the ancestry from which come all things in the world. (4)

17. The Way is like a preface to God. (4)

18. Between the earth and the sky, space is like a bellows, empty yet never spent. (5)

19. In much talk there is great weariness. It is best to keep silent. (5)

20. Heaven is everlasting and the earth is enduring because they do not exist for themselves. (7)

21. The wise man chooses to be last—and is placed first. (7)

22. The highest good, like water, benefits many things, yet occupies dark places men despise. (8)

23. Where there is no strife, there is no blame. (8)

24. The excellence of a house is judged by its site. (8)

25. The excellence of a mind is judged by its wisdom. (8)

26. The excellence of speech is judged by its truthfulness. (8)

27. The excellence of friendship is measured by love. (8)

28. The excellence of a government is judged by its order. (8)

29. The value of an act is judged by its timing. (8)

30. The goal of the Way is peace. (9)

31. To take all one wants is never as good as to stop when one should. (9)

32. Wealth, power, and pride, leave their heritage of doom. (9)

33. Be the chief but never the lord. (10)

34. Thirty spokes unite in the hub, but the worth of the wheel will depend on the void where the axle turns. (11)

35. What gives a clay cup value is the empty space its walls create. (11)

36. Usefulness is to be found in nonexistence. (11)

37. The five colors will blind the eye; the five sounds will deafen the ear; the five flavors will weary the taste; things hard to get will do harm to man's conduct. Therefore the wise will provide for the heart and not for the eye. (12)

38. Favor, like disgrace, brings trouble in its place. (13)

39. One suffers most who is most selfish. (13)

40. He is fit to govern who loves all people as he loves himself. (13)

41. If you hold fast to the Way, you will govern today. (14)

42. The masters of old were much too profound for their times. (15)

43. All things work together and return again each to its roots. (16)

44. The knowledge of loyalty is enlightenment. (16)

45. When you know what is eternal, you know what is righteous. (16)

46. If you know righteousness, though you die, you shall not perish. (16)

47. If you trust people not enough, they may trust you not at all. (17)

48. By not believing a man you turn him into a liar. (17)

49. When shrewdness and cunning appeared, great hypocricy prevailed. (18)

50. When the State is in danger and confused by strife, loyalty becomes the style. (18)

51. Get rid of your preachers and discard your teachers, and the people will benefit a hundredfold. Root out your schemers and renounce your profiteers, and thieving will disappear. (19)

52. Between "yes" and "no" how small the difference; between "good" and "evil" how great the difference. (20)

53. To say, "What all men fear I must fear" is pointless. (20)

54. He who humbles himself shall be preserved; he who bends shall be made straight; he who is empty shall be filled; and he who has little shall succeed. (22)

55. He who is not a competitor, no one in the whole world can compete with him. (22)

56. The ancient proverb, "To remain whole, be twisted," is no idle saying. (22)

57. A hurricane will not outlast the morning and a cloud-burst will not outlast the day. (23)

58. If you work by the Way, you will be of the Way. (23)

59. Little faith is put in those who have little faith. (23)

60. He who raises himself on tiptoe cannot for long remain steady. (24)

61. By your boasting you prove that you have failed. (24)

62. Pride and boasting are like the food of parasites. (24)

63. Be proud and you will never lead. (24)

64. There is something that existed before the earth and the sky began and its name is the Way. (25)

65. Man conforms to the earth; the earth conforms to the sky; the sky conforms to the Way; the Way conforms to its own nature. (25)

66. As the heavy is the foundation of the light, so is repose the foundation of action. (26)

67. How can one be master of ten thousand chariots and still enjoy the glorious view, as all the world may do? (26)

68. A good runner leaves no tracks; and a good speaker makes no blunders. (27)

69. Observe all the white around you, but remember all the black that is there. (28)

70. The greatest carver does little carving; the greatest ruler does little ruling. (28)

71. As for those who would take the whole world to tinker with as they see fit, observe that they never succeed. (29)

72. The wise reject all extremes. (29)

73. Where troops march, there thorns will spring up; and where armies are gathered, there famine will enter. (30)

74. Weapons of war are tools of evil; those who truly admire them are murderers at heart. (31)

75. Those who are on the Way might be compared to rivulets flowing into the sea. (32)

76. He who understands others is wise; he who understands himself is enlightened. (33)

77. He who conquers others is strong; he who conquers his own will is mighty. (33)

78. He who is satisfied with his lot is rich. (33)

79. He who keeps his place endures. (33)

80. The wise man never makes a display of being great, and thus achieves greatness. (34)

81. The great Form is without form; it is nothing to see and nothing to hear, yet it is timeless and endures. (35)

82. If you would take, you must first give, this is the beginning of intelligence. (36)

83. Fish should not be taken out of the water; and weapons should not be rattled before the people. (36)

84. Absence of desires brings tranquillity. (37)

85. The man who does not display his virtue is truly virtuous. (38)

86. True compassion is known by its good deeds. (38)

87. If virtue perishes, charity perishes. (38)

88. A man will eat the fruit, not the flower. (38)

89. A cart is more than the sum of its parts. (39)

90. The nobles and the kings depend upon the lowly for support. (39)

91. It is better to rumble like the common rocks than to tinkle like jade. (39)

92. The great Space has no corners; the great Form has no shape. (40)

93. The Way is nameless and hidden, yet all things gain their fulfillment in it. (41)

94. All things that bear the sun in their arms, bear the shade on their backs. (42)

95. A loss may turn out to be a benefit; and a benefit, a loss. (42)

96. That violent man who does not come to a violent end you may chose as a teacher. (42)

97. The best instruction is not in words. (43)

98. The softest matter in this world penetrates the hardest. (43)

99. A man self-satisfied knows no shame. (44)

100. Gain often hurts more than loss. (44)

101. The stingy man pays the highest price. (44)

102. Perfection is an imperfection. (45)

103. The greatest skill seems like clumsiness; and the greatest eloquence like stuttering. (45)

104. Activity overcomes cold; inactivity overcomes heat: so the wise man by his calm sets everything right in the world. (45)

105. There is no calamity greater than discontent. (46)

106. Where the Way rules, horses are bred for farms; where the Way does not rule, horses are bred for armies. (46)

107. Without leaving the house one may know the entire world; without looking out of the window, one may see the heavens. (47)

108. The wise man knows without moving; he sees without looking; he achieves without doing. (47)

109. The world is lost to those who try to win it. (48)

110. Knowledge is acquired by daily gain; but the Way is acquired by daily loss. (48)

111. The wise hear and see as little children. (49)

112. To the good I would be good, and to the bad I would be good; in that way all might become good. (49)

113. The man who knows how best to be at peace will never meet the tiger or the buffalo that can harm him. (50)

114. All things pay homage to the Way. (51)

115. If you see what is small, you have clearness of vision; if you store up small energies, you gain strength. (52)

116. The great Way is easy to follow, but people wander off on the bypaths. (53)

117. So firm is the Way it cannot be destroyed. (54)

118. Cultivate the Way in the world, and virtue will be universal. (54)

119. With age strength declines; and whatever is contrary to the Way soon ends. (55)

120. They who know do not tell; they who tell do not know. (56)

121. The wise man is moved neither by affection nor hatred, by profit nor loss, by honor nor shame. And for that reason he is held in high esteem by the entire world. (56)

122. Wars are best waged by strategem; but people are best governed by forthrightness. (57)

123. The more prohibitions, the more poverty; the more laws, the more crimes; the more skills, the more luxuries; the more weapons, the more chaos. (57)

124. The wise man says, "When I ask nothing of the people, the people will be honest." (57)

125. Loosen the reins (of government) and the people are happy; tighten the reins, and the people will fret. (58)

126. The wise man is square, but not sharp; straight, but not severe; bright, but not dazzling. (58)

127. In serving Heaven and in ruling men use moderation. (59)

128. Govern a large country as you would fry a small fish (without overdoing it). (60)

129. The great land should practice great humility. (61)

130. Wasn't it said that the seeker will find the Way, and the sinner who finds it will be forgiven? (62)

131. A promise lightly made inspires little confidence. (63)

132. Everything difficult must be dealt with while it is still easy. (63)

133. A thing at rest is easy to hold. (64)

134. Soft things are easy to melt. (64)

135. The time to establish order is before disorder sets in. (64)

136. A thousand-mile journey can be made one step at a time. (64)

137. People are constantly spoiling projects that are only one step from completion. (64)

138. The wise man sets no high value on a thing simply because it is hard to get. (64)

139. The more knowledge the people have, the harder it is to govern them. (65)

140. If you wish to be out front, behave as if you were behind. (66)

141. Three things prize above all: gentleness, frugality and humility. For the gentle can be bold, the frugal can be liberal and the humble can become leaders of men. (67)

142. A good soldier is not pugnacious; and the mighty conqueror does not engage in battle. This is called the pacific virtue. (68)

143. If you cannot advance an inch, retreat a foot. (69)

144. The wise man wears a coarse garment, but carries a jewel in his bosom. (70)

145. To know that one does not know, that is healthy. To think one knows what he does not know, that is a disease. (71)

146. The wise man knows himself, but does not reveal his innermost thoughts. (72)

147. Not in words does God get answers. (73)

148. Where the people do not fear death, nothing is gained by threatening them with death. (74)

149. Where the tax-gatherers grow fat, the people starve. (75)

150. The stiffest tree is readiest for the ax. (76)

151. Man takes from those who have too little and gives it to those who have too much. (77)

152. Nothing is softer than water, yet nothing will alter its way. (78)

153. Everyone knows the paradox that the weak will overcome the strong, and the gentle will prevail in the end. (78)

154. The Way of heaven is impartial; but it favors good men. (79)

155. The ideal land is small, its people few, its tools ten times or even a hundred times beyond their needs. There people live and die and never emigrate. They have weapons and armor that are never used and never displayed. Their food is sweet; their clothes adorned; their homes are at peace, and their customs full of charm. The neighboring lands are so close that each may hear the other's crowing cocks and barking dogs. Yet men grow old and never once exchange a contentious call. (80)

156. It is not good to settle a grievance, if the settlement leads to other grievances. (81)

157. True words may sometimes not sound fine; and fine words may not be true. (81)

158. A good man does not argue. (81)

159. The wise man is not a hoarder. (81)

160. The wise man does his work without contending for the crown. (81)

The Sayings of

ZOROASTRIANISM

On three excellent things be ever
intent: good thoughts, good words,
and good deeds. (*Vendidad XVIII, 17*)

ZOROASTRIANISM

An old religion which no longer has any organized following, such as the Babylonian or Egyptian, is not included among the "living religions." Zoroastrianism is no longer among the vital religions of the world today, since only a handful of people, about one hundred thousand of them, are still followers of this creed, and they follow a form which only remotely resembles ancient Zoroastrianism. But this religion is of interest to us, today, because it had an influence on the great monotheistic religions: Judaism, Christianity and Mohammedanism, and presents us with a record of the earliest groping toward monotheism.

At a time when most religions of the world were animistic and a multiplicity of gods was taken for granted, in ancient Persia there arose a sage, named Spitama Zarathustra, called by the Greeks, Zoroaster, who conceived a new religion. The dates of his birth and death are commonly given as 660 and 583 B.C., though some scholars, with good reason, believe that Zoroaster might have lived many centuries earlier, even as early as 2,000 B.C. Zoroaster systematized the existing beliefs of his primitive people into a new religion which taught that the world and all that is in it was created and ruled over by two forces: Ahura Mazda, the god of all that is good; and Angra Manyu, the god of all that is evil. Ahura Mazda (sometimes translated as "Divine Wisdom") is symbolized in the material world by the three elements: Fire, Water and Earth; with fire the most sacred symbol. So sacred has fire become in the Zoroastrian ritual that its followers have been inaccurately called "Fire Worshipers." Fire, Water and Earth must never be polluted, the Zoroastrian was taught. What pollutes these elements, and the punishment to be meted out to those who so pollute them, is set down in great detail in part of the Zoroastrian sacred scriptures.

Ahura Mazda has six primary attributes, or archangels, through which, or whom, he manifests himself to man. They are: Kindness, Righteousness, Piety, Salvation, Immortality and Sovereignty. And their faithful messenger is Obedience. In addition, of course, Ahura Mazda has many other attributes, sometimes called "sons" and sometimes "angels." And in like manner Zoroastrianism developed a complex demonology, descriptive of the various attributes of Angra Manyu, the god of Death and Evil. These attributes are not outside Ahura Mazda and Angra Manyu, but within them. Yet the section of the sacred scriptures which describes the angels and the demons speaks of them as beings rather than ideas.

Because the sovereignty of the world is so equally divided between Ahura Mazda and Angra Manyu, between Good and Evil, constantly at war with each other, Zoroastrianism has been described as a dualistic religion. But the dualism is seeming rather than real. For Zoroastrianism teaches that after a fixed time Ahura Mazda will defeat and triumph over Angra Manyu, with the aid of all good men who strive to be good, and the world will ultimately be freed from death and evil and forever be ruled only by Ahura Mazda. Zoroastrianism is thus, in its ultimate world view, monotheistic.

The knowledge of the creation and order of the world and its ultimate resolution came to Zoroaster in seven visions. In his thirtieth year he had the first vision, when he was brought before the throne of Ahura Mazda and discoursed with him face to face. During the subsequent ten years he had the remaining six visions. At the end of that time his doctrine was complete. After a long struggle with the priests who opposed him, Zoroaster won over as a convert to his creed King Vishtaspa, and Zoroastrianism was proclaimed the state religion. His creed was simple, practical and kindly. It readily found acceptance by the people, who had apparently just recently domesticated animals and required a discipline suited to rural husbandry. Zoroastrianism, in practice, was such a creed. It served the people well. To be included on the side of Ahura Mazda followers were required to be diligent, truthful, kindly, practice temperance and show respect for all living creatures created by Mazda. Salvation, Zoroaster taught, cannot be brought to any man by priest or teacher; it can come only from within each human being, and for himself. Salvation can be achieved by: *good thoughts*, *good words* and *good deeds*. All the rest is commentary and elaboration.

Zoroastrianism grew and developed in Persia for some centuries. It accumulated a great body of moral teachings, both oral and written. This went on until 330 B.C., when Alexander the Great conquered Persia and destroyed the sacred scriptures of Zoroastrianism. When Persia regained her independence, an organized attempt was made to reconstruct the sacred scriptures of Zoroastrianism from remaining fragments, filled in by the Oral Tradition. Toward the middle of the seventh century A.D., Islam completely overwhelmed Persia and abolished Zoroastrianism and all creeds other than Mohammedanism. Some Persians fled to escape becoming Muslims, and they found refuge in India, where they are known to this day as *Parsees*, or "Persians," and practice, in ever decreasing numbers, a modified form of Zoroastrianism.

Their sacred scriptures are the *Avesta*, or the Law, and to this has been appended the *Zend*, or the Commentary on the Law. Together they are known as the *Zend-Avesta*. The *Avesta* contains mere fragments of the great literature that must have existed earlier, and is divided into five parts: the *Yasna*, or liturgical work, including the *Gathas*, or songs, which are undoubtedly the oldest parts of the *Avesta*; the *Vispered*, which is a later supplement to the *Yasna*; the *Yasht*, the Zoroastrian Psalter; the *Vendidad*, the Zoroastrian Leviticus; and a collection of minor texts of diverse materials. But they do not at present contain anything resembling the Proverbs, though, a priori, such sayings must have existed among the books destroyed by the Greeks, and the books later destroyed by the Muslims.

The sayings included here are principally from the *Venidad*, preceded by a few from the *Gathas*. These sayings are of interest to us because they reflect, with surprising clarity, the teachings of a practical visionary of a very long time ago, who was preoccupied with a good and simple morality rather than a theology; and who addressed himself to a sturdy people in a rugged environment, struggling hard to survive in extremes of climate and to thrive as husbandmen. In such an environment, where the ox and the cow were the ultimate measures of goodness and wealth, and where the faithful shepherd dog was the ultimate in friendship, and of greater value than gold and diamonds, Zoroaster, as reflected in the *Vendidad*, tried to establish as law the practice of generosity, justice, loyalty, cleanliness, purity and, above all, the recognition that "holiness is the best of all good." And holiness, or the Way of Divine Wisdom, is reached through: *Humata, Hakhata, Hvarshta*—the thought well thought; the word well spoken; and the deed well done.

In this one saying the essence of Zoroastrianism is summarized.

The Sayings of
ZOROASTRIANISM

1. What is the thought well thought? It is the thought the holy man thinks and which he holds holy before all other things. What is the word well spoken? It is the word conceived in Reason. What is the deed well done? It is the deed which receives the praise of all who regard righteousness above all. (*Gathas, Yasna* 19:19)

2. Who created me? For whom was I made? Violence and rapine oppressed me and outraged me. I have no other herdsman but You! Prepare for me then the blessings of Your pasture! (*Gathas, Yasna* 29:1)

3. Hear with your ears the best things; look upon them with clear vision; decide between two beliefs, each man for himself, before the Great Consummation. (*Gathas, Yasna* 30:2)

4. If, O Mortals, you observe the commandments that Mazda ordained—of happiness and blessings for the righteous and pain and punishment for the liars—then shall you have bliss hereafter. (*Gathas, Yasna* 30:11)

5. We worship Ahura Mazda who created the cattle, and the waters, and the wholesome plants, the stars, and the earth, and all things that are good. (*Gathas, Yasna* 37:2)

6. May Ahura Mazda by his dominion bring us to work, so that beast and man may prosper; and that we may

through right have familiarity with good thought. (*Gathas, Yasna* 45:9)

7. He is evil who is good to the evil; he is good who is good to the holy and they are his friends. (*Gathas, Yasna* 46:6)

8. Ahura Mazda spoke to Spitama Zarathustra, saying, "I have made every land dear to its people, even though it had no charms whatever in it. Had I not made every land dear to its people, then the whole world would have invaded the Airyana Vaego (Iran)." (*Vd.* I:1)

9. The first of the good lands which Ahura Mazda created was the Airyana Vaego (Iran), whereupon Angra Manyu, who is all death, created the serpent in the river, and winter, a work of the demons. (*Vd.* I:3)

10. Zarathustra asks: "O Maker of the material world, which is the first place where the Earth feels most happy?" And Ahura Mazda replied: "It is the place whereon one of the faithful steps forward." (*Vd.* III:1)

11. "O Maker of the material world, which is the second place where the Earth feels most happy?" "It is one of the places where one of the faithful erects a house with a priest within, with cattle, with a wife, with children; and where the cattle continue to thrive, virtue to thrive, fodder to thrive, the dog to thrive, the wife to thrive, the child to thrive, the fire to thrive, and every blessing of life to thrive." (*Vd.* III:3)

12. "O Maker of the material world, which is the third place where the Earth is most happy?" "It is the place where the faithful grow most corn, grass, and fruit, and

where dry lands are watered and wet lands well drained."
(*Vd.* III:4)

13. "O Maker of the material world, which is the fourth
place where the Earth is most happy?" "It is the place
where flocks and herds most increase." (*Vd.* III:5)

14. "O Maker of the material world, which is the first
place where the Earth feels greatest grief?" "It is the
place where, from the gate of hell, the demons come rushing out." (*Vd.* III:7)

15. "O Maker of the material world, which is the second
place where the Earth feels greatest grief?" "It is the
place where most corpses of dogs and men lie buried."
(*Vd.* III:8)

16. "O Maker of the material world, which is the fifth
place where the Earth feels greatest grief?" "It is the
place where the wife and children of one of the faithful
are driven along the way of captivity, the dry, dusty way,
and lift up their voices in wailing." (*Vd.* III:11)

17. "O Maker of the material world, who is the first to rejoice the Earth with the greatest joy?" "It is he who
cleanses it most of corpses of dogs and men." (*Vd.* III:12)

18. He who does not till the earth with his left arm and
with the right, with the right and the left, to him the
Earth shall say: "O man, ever shall you stand at the door
of the stranger, among those who beg for bread; the
crumbs of the bread will be brought you by those who
have a profusion of wealth." (*Vd.* III:28-29)

19. "What is the food that fills the religious man?" "It is
sowing corn again and again. He who sows corn sows
righteousness." (*Vd.* III:30-31)

20. No one who does not eat has the strength to do heavy works of holiness, of husbandry, strength to beget children. By eating every creature lives, by not eating it dies. (*Vd.* III:33)

21. "O Maker of the material world, if a man should bury in the earth either the corpse of a dog or the corpse of man, and he shall not disinter it within half a year, what is the penalty that he shall pay?" "He shall receive five hundred stripes with the *Aspahe-astra* and five hundred stripes with the *Sraosho-karana.*" (*Vd.* III:36)

22. "O Maker of the material world, if a man should bury in the earth either the corpse of a dog or the corpse of man, and he does not disinter it within two years, what is the penalty that he shall pay?" "For such a deed there is no atonement, nothing that can cleanse it; a trespass for which there is no atonement, forever and ever!" (*Vd.* III:38-39)

23. He who makes a loan without intending to repay it is as one who steals it. (*Vd.* IV:1)

24. "O Maker of the material world, how many in number are your contracts, O Ahura Mazda?" "They are six in number: the word-contract; the hand-contract; the sheep-contract; the ox-contract; the man-contract; the field-contract." (*Vd.* IV:2)

25. "O Maker of the material world, if a man breaks the word-contract, how many of his kin are involved in his sin?" "His sin makes his descendants answerable for three hundred years." (*Vd.* IV:5)

> (Then follow the penalties for all the other contracts, and the terms for which descendants are held answerable for the breach.)

26. If a man rise up with a weapon in his hand, and brandishes it, and he actually smites a man with malicious aforethought, it is: *Aredus* (intent to murder). Upon the fifth *Aredus* he becomes a *Peshotanu* (a murderer). (*Vd.* IV:17)

27. The man who has a wife is far above him who lives in continence; he who keeps a house is far above him who has none; he who has children is far above the childless man; and he who has riches is far above him who has none. (*Vd.* IV:47)

28. Of two men, he who fills himself with food receives good thought much better than he who does not; the former is above him by the worth of a man. (*Vd.* IV:48)

29. Next to life, purity is for man the greatest good. (*Vd.* V:21)

30. Purity is the religion of Mazda, for him who cleanses his soul with good thoughts, good words, and good deeds. (*Vd.* V:21)

31. A weasel does not directly nor indirectly defile any of the creatures of the good spirit, but him who smites and kills it; to him the uncleanliness clings forever and ever. (*Vd.* V:34)

32. "If one's father or mother dies, how long shall they stay in mourning, the son for his father, the daughter for her mother? How long if they were righteous? How long if they were sinners?" "They shall stay thirty days for the righteous and sixty days for the sinners." (*Vd.* XII:1)

(The same question is asked about every conceivable tie of kinship, and the length of mourning is prescribed for each, with double for the sinners.)

33. Whoever shall kill a hedgehog, with the prickly back and the long and thin nose, it is as if he killed his own soul for nine generations." (*Vd*. XIII:3)

34. Whoever shall smite either a shepherd's dog, or a house dog, or a trained dog, his soul, when passing to the other world, shall fly howling louder and more sorely grieved than the sheep in the lofty forest where the wolf ranges. (*Vd*. XIII:8)

> (Then follows praise for every kind of dog, and the punishment for every hurt inflicted upon any of them.)

35. "O Maker of the material world, if a man gives bad food to a shepherd's dog, of what sin does he make himself guilty?" "He makes himself guilty of the same guilt as though he had served bad food to a master of the house of the first rank." (*Vd*. XIII:20)

36. "O Maker of the material world, if there is in the house of a worshiper of Mazda a mad dog that bites without barking, what shall the worshiper do?" "He shall put a wooden collar around the dog's neck, and they shall tie a muzzle to it. If they do not do so, and the dog bites without barking, smites a sheep or wounds a man, they shall pay for the wound of the wounded as for willful murder." (*Vd*. XIII:31)

37. "The dog, I, Ahura Mazda, have made self-clothed and self-shod; watchful and wakeful; sharp-toothed; born to take his food from man, and to watch over man's goods. I have made him strong of body against the evil-doer. And whoever shall awake at his voice, neither shall the thief nor the wolf carry anything from his house without being warned." (*Vd*. XIII:39-40)

38. A dog has the character of eight sorts of people: the priest, the warrior, the husbandman, the strolling singer, the thief, the courtesan and the child. He eats what is left over and is easily satisfied with little, like a priest; he marches in front ready to fight, like a warrior; he is watchful and goes out of the house first, and returns last, like a husbandman; he is ill-trained and changeful, and wounds him who gets too near, like a strolling singer; he prowls around in darkness and is a shameless eater, like a thief; he is fond of singing and roams along the roads like a courtesan; he is fond of sleep, gentle and trusting, and he digs the earth with his paws, like a child. (Vd. XIII:44-48)

39. No house can subsist on earth, made by Ahura, but for the shepherd's dog and the house dog. (Vd. XIII:49)

40. He who kills a water dog brings about a drought that dries up the pasture. (Vd. XIII:52)

41. If any man commits these five sins, and having committed them has not confessed nor atoned for them, he becomes subject to the penalty of two hundred strokes and/or a fine of three hundred istirs:

The first of these is the man who teaches one of the faithful another faith, another law, a lower doctrine, and leads him astray with the full knowledge and conscience of the sin;

The second of these sins is committed when a man feeds a shepherd's dog or a house dog bones too hard or food too hot;

The third sin of these sins is when a man smites a bitch big with young or frightens her by shouting and clapping his hands;

The fourth sin is when a man has intercourse with a woman during her period of impurity;

And the fifth of these sins is when a man has intercourse with a woman who is about to give birth to a child and knows she may come to grief thereby. (*Vd.* XV:2-8)

42. If a man comes near a damsel, either dependent on the chief of the family or not dependent, either delivered to a husband or not delivered, and she conceives by him, let him not, being ashamed of the people, destroy the fruit in her womb. (*Vd.* XV:11)

43. If a man comes near a damsel and she conceives by him, and he says, "Go to the old woman and apply to her for one of her drugs that she may procure the miscarriage," and the damsel does so, the sin is on the head of all three, the man, the damsel, and the old woman. (*Vd.* XV:14)

44. It lies with the faithful to look in the same way after every pregnant female, whether two-footed or four-footed. (*Vd.* XV:19)

45. Atar, the son of Ahura Mazda, watches over a pregnant bitch as well as he does over a pregnant woman. (*Vd.* XV:45)

46. On the three excellent things be ever intent, namely, good thoughts, good words, and good deeds; on the three abominable things be ever on guard, namely, bad thoughts, bad words, and bad deeds. (*Vd.* XVIII:17)

47. When a man of whom the faithful beg does not give anything, be it ever so little, of the riches he has treasured up, that man makes the demons conceive. (*Vd.* XVIII:34-35)

48. When a man, unasked, kindly and piously gives to one of the faithful something, be it ever so little, of the riches he has treasured up, he destroys thereby the offspring of the demons. (*Vd.* XVIII:37-38)

49. Demand of Me that you may be the better, that you may be the happier! (*Vd.* XVIII:60)

50. "O Ahura Mazda! Who grieves you with the sorest grief? Who pains you with the sorest pain?" "It is the courtesan, O Spitama Zarathustra! Verily I say to you, such creatures ought to be killed even as the gliding snake, the howling wolf, or that she-frog that falls upon the water with her thousandfold brood." (*Vd.* XVIII:61-65)

51. By the Word taught by Mazda will I strike, by this Word will I repel the evil-doer, Angra Manyu. (*Vd.* XIX:9)

52. When a man is dead, when his time is over, then the evil-doing demons cut off his eyesight. (*Vd.* XIX:29)

53. The soul enters the way made by Time, and open to both the wicked and the righteous. Then comes the beautiful, well-shaped, strong and well-formed maiden, with the dogs at her sides, the one who can distinguish, who has many children, happy, and of high understanding, and she makes the soul of the righteous go over the Bridge and places that soul in the presence of the heavenly gods themselves. (*Vd.* XIX:28-30)

54. Holiness is the best of all good. (*Vd.* XIX:47)

55. Ahura Mazda brought down the healing plants that by many hundreds, by many thousands, by many myriads, grow up all around. (*Vd.* XX:4)

56. The clouds come from up above down on the earth in thousands of drops, in myriads of drops, to destroy sickness, to destroy death. (*Vd.* XXI:2)

57. If death comes after noon, may healing come in the evening. If death comes in the evening, may healing come in the night. If death comes in the night, may healing come in the morning. (*Vd.* XXI:3)

58. The Holy Word shall keep evil away from you. (*Vd.* XXI:10)

59. The will of the Lord is the law of righteousness. (*Vd.* XXI:22)

Sources for the Sayings of the
TALMUD

(The order or volume is given first, as *Nashim*
(Women) or *Moed* (Holidays), followed by the
tractate or chapter heading, as *Gittin* (Divorces)
or *Kethuboth* (Marriage Documents), followed
by the page number in the Hebrew-Aramaic version of the Babylonian *Talmud*.)

1b. (*Nashim-Sotah*, 32); 2b. (*Nezikin-Sanhedrin*, 49);
3b. (*Nashim-Gittin*, V-8); 4b. (*Moed-Taanith*, 20); 5b.
(*Nezikin-Baba Kamma*, 92); 6b. (*Nashim-Jabamoth*,
105); 7b. (*Moed-Chagegah*, 5); 8b. (*Zeraim-Berachoth*,
24); 9b. (*Zeraim-Berachoth*, 33); 10b. (*Zeraim-Bera-
choth*, 24); 11b. (*Moed-Shabbath*, 104); 12b. (*Nezikin-
Sanhedrin*, 89); 13b. (*Nezikin-Sanhedrin*, 7); 14b.
(*Kodashim-Bechoroth*, LV.6); 15b. (*Nezikin-Shebuoth*,
31); 16b. (*Moed-Taanith*, 7); 17b. (*Kodashim-Bechoroth*, IV-6); 18b. (*Nashim-Kethuboth*, 5); 19b. (*Moed-
Pesachim*, 99); 20b. (*Moed-Pesachim*, 66); 21b. (*Moed-
Megillah*, 182); 22b. (*Nezikin-Sanhedrin*, 7); 23b.
(*Nezikin-Sanhedrin*, 88); 24b. (*Moed-Sukkah*, 49); 25b.
(*Nashim-Gittin*, 7); 26b. (*Nezikin-Baba Bathra*, 10);
27b. (*Nashim-Kethuboth*, 66); 28b. (*Nashim-Sotah*, IX-
15); 29b. (*Moed-Shabbath*, 55); 30b. (*Moed-Sukkah*,
52); 31b. (*Moed-Sukkah*, 52); 32b. (*Moed-Shabbath*,
14); 33b. (*Kodashim-Arachin*, 30); 34b. (*Nezikin-Sanhedrin*, 19); 35b. (*Kodashim-Arachin*, 15); 36b. (*Moed-
Joma*, 43); 37b. (*Moed-Joma*, 86); 38b. (*Zeraim-Berachoth*, IX-5); 39b. (*Nashim-Sotah*, 32); 40b. (*Moed-Eru-*

bin, 100); 41b. (*Zeraim-Berachoth*, 12); 42b. (*Zeraim-Berachoth*, 34); 43b. (*Zeraim-Berachoth*, 55); 44b. (*Moed-Joma*, 86); 45b. (*Nashim-Sotah*, 16); 46b. (*Moed-Pesachim*, 113); 47b. (*Nashim-Kiddushin*, 40); 48b. (*Zeraim-Berachoth*, 29); 49b. (*Moed-Pesachim*, 113); 50b. (*Nashim-Nedarim*, 39); 51b. (*Nashim-Sotah*, 31); 52b. (*Zeraim-Berachoth*, 34); 53b. (*Moed-Shabbath*, II-5); 54b. (*Moed-Betzah*, 32); 55b. (*Nezikin-Baba Metzia*, 38); 56b. (*Moed-Shabbath*, 32); 57b. (*Nezikin-Sanhedrin*, 19); 58b. (*Nashim-Nedarim*, 62); 59b. (*Moed-Shabbath*, 119); 60b. (*Nashim-Kiddushin*, 40); 61b. (*Moed-Chagigah*, 5); 62b. (*Moed-Pesachim*, 3); 63b. (*Moed-Erubin*, 54); 64b. (*Nezikin-Baba Bathra*, 21); 65b. (*Nashim-Gittin*, 58); 66b. (*Moed-Koton*, 9); 67b. (*Moed-Megillah*, 14); 68b. (*Moed-Megillah*, 14); 69b. (*Moed-Shabbath*, 33); 70b. (*Nashim-Kiddushin*, 49); 71b. (*Nashim-Kethuboth*, 65); 72b. (*Nashim-Kethuboth*, 30); 73b. (*Nashim-Kethuboth*, 65); 74b. (*Moed-Megillah*, 14); 75b. (*Teharoth-Niddah*, 45); 76b. (*Nezikin-Baba Metzia*, 59); 77b. (*Nezikin-Sanhedrin*, 22); 78b. (*Nezikin-Baba Metzia*, 59); 79b. (*Nashim-Jabamoth*, 62); 80b. (*Moed-Joma*, I-1); 81b. (*Nashim-Jabamoth*, 63); 82b. (*Nashim-Kiddushin*, 70); 83b. (*Moed-Pesachim*, 49); 84b. (*Kodashim-Chullin*, 84); 85b. (*Moed-Shabbath*, 10); 86b. (*Nashim-Gittin*, 6); 87b. (*Nezikin-Sanhedrin*, 22); 88b. (*Nezikin-Baba Metzia*, 86); 89b. (*Nezikin-Baba Metzia*, 86); 90b. (*Nezikin-Sanhedrin*, IV-5); 91b. (*Moed-Pesachim*, 113); 92b. (*Nezikin-Sanhedrin*, 29); 93b. (*Nashim-Nedarim*, 49); 94b. (*Nashim-Kethuboth*, V-5); 95b. (*Nezikin-Baba Metzia*, 71); 96b. (*Zeraim-Berachoth*, 40); 97b. (*Nezikin-Avodah Zorah*, 20); 98b. (*Nezikin-Baba Kamma*, 92); 99b. (*Moed-Joma*, 63); 100b. (*Nezikin-Baba Metzia*, 59); 101b. (*Moed-Shabbath*, 31).

Selected Bibliography

Wisdom literature, in general, is as old as it is vast. Aristotle was the author of a collection of proverbs. But already in his day there existed diverse collections of fables, maxims and sayings of different origins and in different languages. The Proverbs of Solomon and the Sayings of Ben Sirach, the maxims of the *Jatakas* and the *Hitopadesa*, and the moral conclusions of the collected fables attributed to Aesop were already in existence in Aristotle's day. These were followed by similar collections by Hesiod and Homer, Pindar and Solon, Meander and Plato, and many others; and they have continued to multiply throughout the centuries, through Lydgate, Cato, Erasmus, Taverner, Camden, Lord Bacon, Herbert, Fuller, and a host of others, all the way to Benjamin Franklin who preserved and created some of his own sayings in "Poor Richard's Almanac." The vastness of this literature might be realised by glancing through the bibliography in two large volumes, called *Katalog Bernsteina*, which lists and describes 4761 collections of proverbs in the library of Ignace Bernstein. Though the Bernstein library is considered the largest single collection of collections of proverbial literature, it is far from definitive. And among the early collections of wisdom literature many are religious in nature and in origin and are to be found in the Sacred Books of the world.

Therefore anyone eager to explore the areas treated in the present volume will find abundant material in almost any good library. And it will be found that most books on comparative religion and on the wisdom literature of any specific religion contain bibliographies for further exploration.

Here is a brief list of annotated books as a starting point for the general reader:

The Religions of Mankind, Edmund Davidson Soper; Abigdon-Cokesbury, New York, 1921. A good general introduction to the entire topic of comparative religion.

How the Great Religions Began, Joseph Gaer; Dodd, Mead & Co., New York, revised edition, 1956. The world's living religions presented concisely in terms of the lives, beliefs, and teachings of their founders.

The Bible of Mankind, Mizra Ahmad Sohrab; Universal Pub. Co., New York, 1929.

The World's Great Scriptures, Lewis Browne; Macmillan, New York, 1946.

The Scriptures of Mankind, Charles Samuel Braden; Macmillan, New York, 1952. These are excellent collections of selections from the world's sacred books; and each has its own advantages. The Sohrab book contains excellent if brief introductions to the several religions treated; the Browne book contains the best selections; and the Braden book is particularly useful because of his instructive general introduction and his annotated bibliography on each of the religions he treats.

The Sacred Books of the East, (50 Volumes), edited by Max Muller; The Clarendon Press, Oxford, published over a period of several years at the end of the last century. Highly scholarly, but highly rewarding translations of the best works of all the eastern religions by the most reputable and skillful scholars in their respective fields. Selections from these books have also been published in a 14-volume set. Many of the translations of individual books have appeared separately.

The Teachings of the Compassionate Buddha, edited by E. A. Burtt; New American Library, New York, 1955. This volume, in a paperbound edition, is an excellent introduction to a very complex topic about which there still exists too little knowledge in the Western world. It contains also a version of "The Dhammapada."

The Dhammapada, translated by Irving Babbitt; Oxford University Press, New York, 1936. In addition to the translation of "The Dhammapada," of which there are many translated versions, this volume contains a stimulating essay on the Buddha and the Occident.

Jatakas, translated and edited by E. B. Cowell; Cambridge University Press, Edinburgh and London, 1895. The only comprehensive translation of the 550 Jatakas in English (6 volumes); most subsequent collections and version are based on it or are derived from it.

The Growth of the Gospels, Frederick C. Grant; The Abington Press, New York, 1933. Though intended for the student, this book is written so that any layman can read it with ease, enjoyment, and profit.

The Parables of the Synoptic Gospels, B. T. D. Smith; Cambridge University Press, London, 1937. A good book for anyone who wishes to have a better understanding of the parables of the Synoptic Gospels and their historical background.

The Lore of the New Testament, Joseph Gaer; Little, Brown & Co., Boston, 1952. A biography of Jesus as it appears in folk imagination; with the lore of the apostles.

The Story of Confucius, Brain Brown; David McKay, Philadelphia, 1927. A biography of Confucius and a discussion of his ethics; illustrated with many of his best-known sayings which are necessary to an understanding of Confucianism.

The Wisdom of Confucius, Lin Yutang; Modern Library, New York, 1938. This is as good an introduction to Confucius and his teachings as can be found between the covers of a single volume.

Hinduism, L. D. Barrett; Open Court Pub., Chicago (no date of publication given). This brief essay in almost outline form gives the progression in the development of Hinduism from the Vedic Age to the sects of the 19th century.

The Song Celestial, (The Bhagavad Gita), translated from the Sanskrit by Sir Edwin Arnold; Roberts, Boston, 1895. There are today a number of translations of this far-famed poem, but none excell Sir Arnold's version.

Hitopadesa: The Book of Wholesome Councel, translated by Francis Johnson; revised by Lionel D. Barnett; Chapman and Hall, London, 1923.

Hitopadesa or the Book of Good Councel, translated from the Sanskrit by B. Hale-Wortham; Routlege, London, (no publication date given). Both of these books are easy to read and rewarding; both contain explanatory material of interest to the lay reader.

Indian Thought and Its Development, Albert Schweitzer; Holt, New York, 1936. This book contains as good an introduction to the teachings of Jainism as will be found anywhere.

Everyman's Talmud, A. Cohen; E. P. Dutton, New York, 1949. A comprehensive summary of the basic teachings of the Talmud prepared for the lay reader; with a good introduction explaining the historical backgrounds of the Talmud and its formation.

The Lore of the Old Testament, Joseph Gaer; Little, Brown and Co., Boston, 1951. A vast collection of extra-canonical stories arranged in sequence to present the characters and events that appear in the Hebrew Scriptures.

Sayings of the Fathers, translated by Joseph H. Hertz; Behrman House, New York, 1945. The late Chief Rabbi of the British Empire presents here in parallel columns the Hebrew and the English text of the Sayings of the Fathers, and annotates them with an excellent running commentary.

Mohammedanism: A Historical Survey, H. A. R. Gibb; Oxford University Press, London, 1949; made available in a paperbound edition (A Mentor Book) in 1955. This gives a bird's-eye-view of Mohammedanism from its inception to the present day; and is appended by a bibliography of seventy-seven books for the reader enticed to explore the topic more thoroughly.

The Sayings of Mohammed, Allama Sir Abdulah Al-Manum Al-Suhrwady; The Wisdom of the East series; John Murray, London, 1941. A fairly large collection of Sayings from accepted Hadith sources, from which 159 have been adapted and included in this book.

The Short Koran, edited by George M. Lamsa; Ziff-Davis Pub. Co., Chicago, 1949. Selections from the Koran, topically arranged. A good book for those who have never tried to read the Koran in its entirety.

Modern Japan and Shinto Nationalism, D. C. Holtom; University of Chicago Press, Chicago, 1943. A brief but lucid discussion of Shintoism as a State Religion by a notable authority on the topic and the author of a number of books on Japan and its native religion.

The Old Fellow, Herryman Maurer; John Day, New York, 1943. A lively and humourous story of Lao-Tze, the obscure founder of Taoism, which reads like a novel, but is atheticated and scholarly.

The Sayings of Lao Tzu, Lionel Giles; Wisdom of the East series; American Edition, E. P. Dutton, New York, 1908. A splendid collection of sayings from the Tao-Te-King.

The Ethical Religion of Zoroaster, Miles Meander Dawson; Macmillan, New York, 1931. A biography of Zoroaster, with an analysis of his ethics; contains also a comparison of Zoroaster's sayings with those found in Judaism and Christianity.

Topical Index

Accord, see: *Discord*

ADULTERY

Bud. 5, 150a, 151a
Chr. 11
Jud. TCA, 63
Moh. 7a, 8a, 9a
Zor. 42, 43

Admonition, see: *Correction*
Affliction, see: *Sorrow*

AGE

Bud. 58a, 72a
Jud. 8, 98c
Moh. 10a

Aid, see: *Protection*
Allah, see: *God*
Ambition, see: *Desire*

ANGER

Bud. 112a, 115a, 116a, 72b
Chr. 122, 139, 16a
Jai. 73

BROTHERHOOD
(Unity)

Chr. (Parable 22, 26) 31, 45, 55, 62, 66, 74, 86, 90, 121, 128, 163, 8a, 10a
Con. 94, 137
Hin. 61, 66, 26a, 55a
Jai. 14, 69
Jud. 7, 47, 237, 238
Moh. 57, 3a, 54a, 57a, 64a, 71a, 77a, 78a, 94a
Sh. 36, 50, 45
Tao. 40, 112

Calm, see: *Serenity*

CHARITY
(Benevolence, Generosity)

Bud. 6, 116a, 125a, 63b
Chr. 91, 110, 111, 113, 117, 7a, 12a
Con. 25, 30, 50
Hin. 126, 127, 128, 31a, 59a
Jud. 10, 11, 20, 53, 78, 135, 206, 22a, 24b, 25b, 26b, 16c
Moh. 19, 21, 44, 60, 11a, 12a, 13a, 14a, 15a, 22a, 24a, 70a, 90a
Tao. 87, 151
Zor. 47, 48

Chastisement, see: *Retribution*
Children, see: *Parents*

COMMANDMENTS

Bud. 1, 2, 3, 4, 5, 6
Chr. 62
Jud. TC
Moh. 1, 2, 34
Zor. 1

COMPANIONSHIP
(Association)

Bud. 35a, 105a, 106a, 148a, 158a, 159a, 43b, 82b, 97b

TAO. 46
ZOR. 9, 52, 56, 57

DECEPTION
(Hypocrisy)
BUD. 5, 38b, 49b
CHR. 33, 159, 13a
JAI. 48
JUD. TC, 134, 153, 168, 48b, 80c
MOH. 56
SH. 12, 44
TAO. 49, 60
ZOR. 23

DEEDS
BUD. 31a, 39a, 41a, 65a, 73a, 88a, 19b, 25b
CHR. 34, 35, 93, 109, 140, 143, 144 (Par. 17)
CON. 1, 39, 95, 125
HIN. 13, 14, 16, 28, 29, 35, 41a, 81a
JAI. 11, 17, 18, 60
JUD. 13a, 15a, 34a, 45a, 50a, 55a, 60a, 24c
MOH. 67, 24a, 60a
TAO. 11, 147
ZOR. 1

DESIRE
(Ambition, Indulgence, Lust, Passion)
BUD. 8a, 95a, 101a, 110a, 139a, 140a, 146a, 162a, 164a, 165a, 167a,
    169a, 173a, 180a, 8b, 50b, 86b, 88b, 92b
CHR. 138
CON. 147
HIN. 22, 27, 40, 47, 63, 108, 110, 112, 118, 119, 139, 21a
JAI. 74
JUD. 58, 143, 200, 24a
MOH. 157a
TAO. 5

Discontent, see: *Contentment*

DISCORD
(Accord, Contention, Strife)
BUD. 4a, 12b
CHR. 40
CON. 24, 42
JUD. 111, 166, 229
MOH. 51a
SH. 22
TAO. 13, 23, 50

Divorce, see: *Marriage and Divorce*

DOUBT
(Indecision, Uncertainty)
BUD. 74a, 169a
CHR. 114, 135, 136
CON. 86
HIN. 55
JUD. 8c
SH. 37

DRUNKENNESS
BUD. 5
JUD. 148, 186, 47b, 76c
MOH. 28, 55a

DUTY
BUD. 6, 85a, 36b
CON. 4, 102
HIN. 9, 32, 34, 39
JAI. 27
JUD. 28a
MOH. 139a
SH. 5, 32

EDUCATION
(Teaching, Study)
BUD. 93a, 94a, 46b, 62b, 83b
CON. 4, 16, 17, 18, 57, 58, 61, 64, 66, 68, 74, 87, 130, 142

TAO. 6, 22, 45, 46, 52, 87, 95, 118, 154, 155
ZOR. 7, 19, 27, 46, 59

GOSSIP
BUD. 91b
CON. 153, 156
JAI. 28
JUD. 108, 4a, 77c

GOVERNMENT
(Leaders, Rulers)
CON. 14, 21, 97, 108, 109, 110, 119, 145, 148, 164
JAI. 41
JUD. 180, 181, 30a, 50c
MOH. 51
SH. 7, 12, 13, 14, 16, 17, 18, 28, 32
TAO. 15, 28, 40, 50, 70, 90, 122, 123, 125, 128, 139, 148, 149

GREED
(Avarice, Miserliness)
BUD. 115a, 172a, 76b
CHR. 131
CON. 35, 37, 71, 76
HIN. 11, 18a, 60a, 61a
JUD. 174, 196, 235
MOH. 64, 20a, 50a, 119a
TAO. 71, 101

Grief, see: *Sorrow*
Guest, see: *Hospitality*
Guilt, see: *Evil*

HAPPINESS
(Joy, Pleasure)
BUD. 5, 23a, 76a, 102a, 144a, 5b, 37b, 53b
CHR. 5a
CON. 63, 146
HIN. 141, 142, 6a, 56a, 66a, 100a

MEDITATION
(Contemplation)
Bud. 4, 1a, 14a, 91a, 107a, 138a, 147a, 179a
Hin. 11
Jai. 27, 47, 61, 78
Moh. 107a
Sh. 15

MERCY
(Compassion, Pity)
Bud. 11b, 44b
Chr. 6, 30a
Hin. 30a
Jud. 227, 10c, 71c, 116c
Moh. 23, 65, 79a, 82a, 127a
Tao. 86

Miserliness, see: Greed

MODERATION
(Excess)
Bud. 5, 22b, 93b
Chr. 123
Con. 11, 28, 56, 73, 90, 92, 131, 150
Hin. 62, 68
Jai. 63
Tao. 31, 72, 102, 127

MODESTY
Jai. 76
Moh. 122a, 123a
Tao. 85, 140

Mourning, see: Sorrow

MURDER
Bud. 4, 5, 69a
Jai. 34, 51, 55

SLANDER

Bud. 4
Chr. 132, 152
Con. 96
Jud. 39
Moh. 68, 5a, 18a, 41a, 65a, 67a

SPEECH
(Words)

Bud. 4, 31a, 128a, 69b
Chr. 43, 44, 125, 143, 149, 150
Con. 39, 43, 107, 120, 125, 144, 163
Jud. 25, 29, 107, 123, 156, 12a, 31a, 67b, 28c, 49c, 73c, 84c, 109c, 110c
Moh. 73a, 90a
Tao. 26, 68, 157

SORROW
(Grief, Pain, Mourning, Suffering)

Bud. 1, 2, 3, 51a, 102a, 108a, 37b, 67b, 75b, 85b
Chr. 3, 32
Con. 161
Hin. 51a, 100a
Jai. 19, 83
Jud. 23, 84, 91, 122, 160, 7b, 15c, 38c
Moh. 11
Tao. 38, 57, 94
Zor. 14, 15, 16, 32

Strife, see: *Discord*
Study, see: *Education*
Suffering, see: *Sorrow*
Teaching, see: *Education*

TEMPTATION

Bud. 5a, 22a, 28a, 55b
Chr. 137, 15a

USURY
JUD. 177, 94b
JOH. 149a

Virtue, see: *Good*

WAR
CON. 118
JAI. 36
JUD. 30, 68a
MOH. 13
TAO. 73, 74, 83

WEALTH
(Riches)
BUD. 3b
CHR. 18, 20, 50, 56
CON. 12, 62, 122
HIN. 48a, 69a, 78a
JUD. 7, 75, 102, 120, 125, 145, 20a, 52c, 58c, 62c, 74c
MOH. 141a, 142a
TAO. 32
ZOR. 27

WISDOM
(Insight, Perception, Wise man)
BUD. 6, 15a, 16a, 17a, 18a, 19a, 30a, 37a, 38a, 48a, 59a, 120a, 166a, 178a
CHR. (Par. 1, 3, 4, 5, 13, 20); 10, 38, 105
CON. 20, 34, 47, 55, 81, 103, 106, 111, 114, 116, 123, 126, 135, 156, 165
HIN. 1, 18, 19, 26, 56, 103, 107, 115, 2a, 3a, 12a, 22a, 23a, 44a, 63a, 71a, 77a, 78a, 89a, 93a
JAI. 1, 25, 54, 66, 79
JUD. 28, 33, 48, 104, 106, 149, 190, 199, 204, 11a, 17a, 18a, 46a, 58a, 67a, 4b, 39b, 1c, 2c, 4c, 5c, 20c, 87c, 88c, 92c, 99c, 123c
MOH. 118a, 136a

Index

SCHOOLCRAFT
COLLEGE LIBRARY

Dhammapadaŋ

I. YAMAKAVAGGO.

1. Manopubbaṅgamā dhammā manoseṭṭhā manomayā,
   manasā ce paduṭṭhena bhāsati[1] vā karoti vā,
   tato naŋ dukkhaṁ anveti cakkaŋ va vahato padaŋ.

   1. Cakkhupâlatthera-vatthu, I, 8.

2. Manopubbaṅgamā dhammā manoseṭṭhā manomayā,
   manasā ce pasannena bhāsati vā karoti vā,
   tato naŋ sukham anveti chāyā va anapāyinī.

   2. Maṭṭakuṇḍali-vatthu, I, 25.

3. " Akkocchi maŋ, avadhi maŋ, ajini maŋ, ahāsi me "
   ye[2] taŋ upanayhanti,[3] veraŋ tesaŋ na sammati.

4. " Akkocchi maŋ, avadhi maŋ, ajini maŋ, ahāsi me "
   ye[2] taŋ na[4] upanayhanti,[3] veraŋ tesūpasammati.[5]

   3. Tissatthera-vatthu, I, 37.

[1] F. bhāsati.   [2] B[r] ye ca.
[3] F. upanayihanti; B[r], S[c], K. upanayhanti.
[4] B[r] nūpanayhanti; S[c] nopanayhanti.
[5] B[r] tesaŋ upasammati.

1[b]. Cf. A. i, 11 (I, vi, 6, 7); Maitr. Br. Up. VI,
34 ; Netti, 129, 133.
2[e]. Tha. 1041-3.
3-6. Vin. i, 349; Jāt. iii, 212 (108-10).

1

First page of the *Dhammapada* transliterated from Pali, the sacred language of Buddhist Scriptures

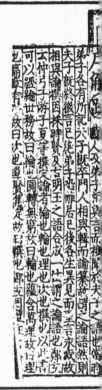

First page of a prayer in Chinese, a collection

An illuminated title page of the *Koran*, the Sacred Scriptures of Islam, (in Arabic).